THE BOOK OF THE SEVENTH ROYAL INNISKILLING FUSILIERS

LIEUT.-COLONEL H. N. YOUNG, D.S.O., The Royal Inniskilling Fusiliers.
Killed in Action—France, October 25th, 1918.

THE BOOK

OF

The Seventh Service Battalion

The Royal Inniskilling Fusiliers

FROM

TIPPERARY TO YPRES

BY

G. A. COOPER WALKER

Dublin:

BRINDLEY & SON, PRINTERS, EUSTACE STREET

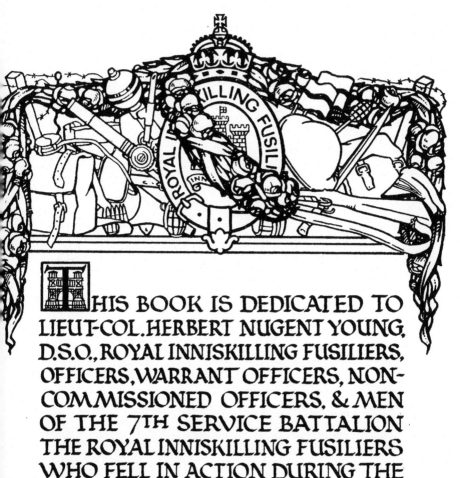

THIS BOOK IS DEDICATED TO LIEUT-COL. HERBERT NUGENT YOUNG, D.S.O., ROYAL INNISKILLING FUSILIERS, OFFICERS, WARRANT OFFICERS, NON-COMMISSIONED OFFICERS, & MEN OF THE 7TH SERVICE BATTALION THE ROYAL INNISKILLING FUSILIERS WHO FELL IN ACTION DURING THE GREAT WAR.

This is a memorial of their honour and of our gratitude. Let us be zealous to emulate them, and, judging that happiness is freedom, and freedom is valour, see to it that their names be not forgotten.

EVERYWHERE AND ALWAYS FAITHFUL

CONTENTS

PREFACE

The book of the 7th (S) Battalion Royal Inniskilling Fusiliers, laid before you in the following chapters, deals with the training and movements of the unit from its formation, in October, 1914, to August 26th, 1917, the date of its amalgamation with the 8th Battalion.

The incidents related are compiled from the "War Diary," Battalion orders, records and personal memoirs, and are set out, to the best of my ability and belief, in correct chronological and historical order.

In writing the narrative I took special care to avoid matters which might lead to political, military, or religious controversy.

To enliven the monotony of mere history I have inserted a few anecdotes and humorous stories which, I trust, will cause no ill-feeling to those concerned—in practically every case I obtained the permission of those mentioned. Unnecessary details have been omitted, and I have endeavoured to give space to events in proportion to their importance. I had hoped that the history of our training at home might have been recorded more fully, but lack of sufficient data and a somewhat lethargic memory in matters of routine have prevented me from doing this. The general outline now submitted deals with the salient points only.

Throughout the book I have made references to many officers and other ranks—in all cases I did so in the rank in which they were serving at the period they are mentioned.

My chief regret has been that I was unable to do justice to so many of the deeds of individual N.C.O's. and men, but in a unit where the personnel were constantly changing, as a result of casualties and sickness, it was impossible to keep pace with this and record the changes minutely.

As Signal Officer to the battalion for nearly two and a-half years, I was placed in the unique position—especially on active service—of hearing and seeing many things which did not come within the scope of all. Through the vicissitudes of active service I have tried to depict our life as it was, and, I hope, without favour or partiality.

If I have succeeded in drawing a picture of the life of the unit during the first three years of the war, then I shall feel gratified and amply repaid for the time and trouble expended.

With the approval and consent of the Committee of the Battalion Memorial Fund the book is dedicated to the memory of our late commanding officer, Lieut.-Colonel H. N. Young, D.S.O., officers, warrant officers, non-commissioned officers and men who were killed in action and died of wounds.

In conclusion, I wish to tender my warm appreciation for the way in which so many officers, other ranks, and friends of " The Seventh " assisted me, financially, to publish the book ; indeed, had it not been for their help it would have been quite impossible to have carried the work through. My special thanks are due to General Sir Archibald J. Murray, G.C.M.G., etc., Colonel-in-Chief of the regiment, for his patronage and contribution in the form of a Foreword ; to Major-General Sir W. B. Hickie, K.C.B., late G.O.C. 16th (Irish) Division, for writing the introduction to our life " on active service " ; to Lieut.-Colonel Michael Hughes for his liberal financial donation ; to Mrs. H. N. Young for lending me the personal and most valued records of our late commanding officer ; to Major V. H. Parr, D.S.O., M.C., for his great assistance and advice throughout the work ; to Captain C. H. Stainforth, M.C. ; Major Sir Robert Lynch-Blosse, Bart ; Lady Lynch-Blosse, Captain G. O. F. Alley, M.C., R.A.M.C. ; C.Q.M.S. J. Louden, J. A. L., Mrs. Michael Hughes, Captain H. W. Ruddock, Cadet R. L. D. Maunsell, Captain G. Le Fevre, Captain A. E. C. Trimble, Lieut. T. E. Johnston (Editor " Sprig of Shillelagh ") and others for their help and support.

Acknowledgments are also due, for copyright and permission to reproduce illustrations, etc., to the Imperial War Museum, the Editor " Irish Life " and H.M. Stationery Office, Dublin.

G. A. C. W.

Dublin,
    26th August, 1920.

LIST OF ABBREVIATIONS

C.-IN-C.	..	Commander-in-Chief.
G.O.C.	..	General Officer Commanding.
C.O.	..	Commanding Officer.
BDE. HQRS.	..	Brigade Headquarters.
BN. HQRS.	..	Battalion Headquarters.
S.A.A.	..	Small Arms Ammunition.
G.H.Q.	..	General Headquarters.
L. OF C.	..	Lines of Communication.
T.M.B.	..	Trench Mortar Battery.
R.F.A.	..	Royal Field Artillery.
M/G.	..	Machine Gun.
C.C.S.	..	Casualty Clearing Station.
L.T.M.B.	..	Light Trench Mortar Battery.
N.C.O.	..	Non-Commissioned Officer.
W.O.	..	Warrant Officer.
COY.	..	Company.
C.T.	..	Communication Trench.
" G "	..	General Staff.
" Q "	..	Quartermaster's Staff.
S.P.	..	Strong Point.
C.S.M.	..	Company Sergeant-Major.
R.S.M.	..	Regimental Sergeant-Major.
P.U.O.	..	Trench Fever.
O.P.	..	Observation Post.
U.K.	..	United Kingdom.
R.T.O.	..	Railway Transport Officer.
A.P.M.	..	Assistant Provost-Marshal.
A.M.L.O.	..	Assistant Military Landing Officer.
F.P.	..	Field Imprisonment
M.O.	..	Medical Officer.
A.A.A.	..	Full Stop (Telegraphic).

LIST OF ILLUSTRATIONS

(All illustrations in this book are copyright, the property of the author.)

(Blocks by the Irish Photo Engraving Co.)

PART I.

FOREWORD

BY

GENERAL SIR ARCHIBALD J. MURRAY

G.C.M.G., K.C.B., C.V.O., D.S.O., Grand Officer Legion of Honour, etc.

Late Chief of the Imperial General Staff.
Colonel, The Royal Inniskilling Fusiliers.

The first to command the 7th Battalion was that fine soldier, Colonel R. C. C. Cox. An Inniskilling, and an officer of ripe experience, tact, and sound judgment, I feel sure that the 7th Battalion owed much to his patient work. Lieutenant-Colonel H. N. Young, D.S.O., with whom the fighting history of the battalion is inseparably connected, was one of the finest fighting soldiers the war produced. A soldier of exceptional physique, he knew no fear. The harder the fighting, the greater the difficulty of the situation, the more he rose to the occasion and stood out as a commander to be relied on. Many a general has told me how implicitly they relied on him when fighting was going on. On the 13th October, 1918, so near to the end of the war, he fell in action, but will live in the memory of the Regiment for all time.

This little history tells the tale of the gallantry and devotion to duty of Lieutenant-Colonel A. D. Reid, D.S.O., and Major R. G. Kerr, M.C., whose names are inscribed on the Roll of Honour with their comrades who gave their lives, unhesitatingly, for God, King and Country.

I trust that this Book of the Seventh Service Battalion of the Royal Inniskilling Fusiliers will take a prominent place in the libraries of the remaining battalions of the regiment. Here, I feel sure, it will be handled with reverence and affection by generations of Inniskillings. For myself, I feel proud to have my name associated with this Service Battalion of glorious memory.

ARCHIBALD MURRAY,

General.

Colonel, Royal Inniskilling Fusiliers.

Weni House,
West Malling,
Kent.
October, 1920.

FOREWORD

→§·§←

As Colonel of the Royal Inniskilling Fusiliers, a regiment I joined in 1879, I feel that I and all my brother officers, past and present, of the old " Inniskillings " owe a deep debt of gratitude to this splendid 7th Battalion for the honour and glory it has brought to the dear old Regiment.

As I read this narrative of wonderful events, so simply and effectively told, the first thought that comes to my mind is how nobly the 7th Battalion Royal Inniskilling Fusiliers, during its life of three years, acted up to the motto of the Regiment—" Nec aspera terrent." The narrative lays no undue stress on the hardships, endured cheerfully, without a murmur or the slightest loss of discipline—hardships often so great that the actual battle was perhaps the easier part of war.

It seems to me as if the officers, non-commissioned officers and men continually had in remembrance that the honour and fair fame of the old regiment, with its history dating back to 1689, was in their hands, and they determined never to forget it, and they never did.

No foreign nation, certainly not the Germans, believed that we could put an entirely new army into the field, trained, equipped and disciplined, in less than a year. This we did. The task would have been harder, perhaps impossible, if we had not had the old army with its traditions to serve as a model and example to the new army. It is world knowledge how well the work was done. The 16th (Irish) Division was a fine example of this new army, and won a glorious reputation, the remembrance of which will never die. The G.O.C. bears respected testimony to the worth and good work of the 7th Battalion Royal Inniskilling Fusiliers.

CHAPTER I.

IN TRAINING (IRELAND).

General outline of formation of Division and commands—The origin of the battalion—Arrival in Tipperary—Colonel R. C. C. Cox assumes command—Outline of early training—The lack of recruits—Move to Scalaheen Camp—Departure of the C.O.—Lieutenant-Colonel Michael Hughes assumes command—Formation of sports committee and general recreations of the unit—The withdrawal of three hundred men as a draft for 10th Division—Subsequent recruiting campaigns—The regimental sports on August 2nd, 1915—Finner Camp and inspection by G.O.C.—Results of training and recruiting activities in Ulster—Departure to England on 8th September, 1915.

In accordance with Army Council Instructions, and the approval of His Majesty King George V., the 16th (Irish) Division was formed on, or about, the 14th September, 1914.

Lieutenant-General Sir Lawrence Parsons, K.C.B., assumed command of the division, and made his temporary headquarters in Dublin. In October the G.O.C. and his staff moved to Mallow, which place afterwards became the permanent site of his command.

Representative battalions of every Irish infantry regiment went to make up the units of the newly-formed Division, which consisted of the 47th, 48th and 49th Infantry Brigades.

The 49th Infantry Brigade was formed on the 1st October, 1914, and Brigadier-General R. Douglas Longe was appointed to command it. The headquarters of the Brigade was established in Tipperary barracks, and during the ensuing week the four battalion cadres moved in and occupied the barracks, together with a portion of the " Union " as extra accommodation.

A

The battalions formed to comprise the 49th Infantry Brigade were :—

> The 7th ("S") Battalion Royal Inniskilling Fusiliers.
> The 8th ("S") Battalion Royal Inniskilling Fusiliers.
> The 7th ("S") Battalion Royal Irish Fusiliers.
> The 8th ("S") Battalion Royal Irish Fusiliers.

On the 2nd October, 1914, the battalion was formed with six officers and eighteen other ranks under Second-Lieutenant T. Olphert, who arrived from Dublin on that date. A nucleus of ex-W.O.'s and N.C.O.'s accompanied the party to form an instructional staff. Colour-Sergeant Kearney, Sergeant Taylor, Corporal Dolan and several others were among those selected. For the next week, every day saw new arrivals at the barracks. Recruits arrived in small parties, and many new army officers, just commissioned, were posted to the Brigade. A proportion of these were posted to the strength of "The Seventh." By mutual understanding, for the first few days Second-Lieutenant T. Olphert acted as C.O. of the battalion, and Second-Lieutenant E. J. McCormick officiated in the capacity of adjutant.

By the 5th inst. Major R. Lynch-Blosse—a retired regular officer who had served in the K.O.S.B.—was posted to the battalion, and took over command.

On the 8th October, Colonel R. C. C. Cox, Royal Inniskilling Fusiliers, arrived and assumed command. Our new C.O. joined the 27th Inniskillings on 21st June, 1879, served in the South African War, was mentioned in despatches, and received the Queen's Medal with five clasps. He commanded the 2nd Battalion Royal Inniskilling Fusiliers 1904-1908. Major Lynch-Blosse was appointed second-in-command, with effect from this date.

"The Seventh," which only a week before had been a mere cadre, was now twenty-three officers and about 350 other ranks strong. So far, at any rate, recruiting was progressing favourably, and by the end of the month it became just possible to form the battalion into companies and platoons. The original four companies were commanded as follows :—

> "A" Company—Second-Lieutenant W. H. Collis.
> "B" Company—Captain A. H. Ommaney.
> "C" Company—Second-Lieutenant T. Olphert.
> "D" Company—Major M. J. Kenny.

Captain W. R. R. Roe was appointed acting-adjutant, and Second-Lieutenant J. J. L. Gibson in the position of quarter-master.

These commands were only temporarily authorised by the C.O., and by the beginning of November Captain Roe was given the command of "A" Company, and Second-Lieutenant J. J. L. Gibson was appointed adjutant.

By the end of October the barracks was almost full. Nearly 1,800 men had joined the Brigade, and over a hundred officers. The accommodation, which in peace time would have been just enough for an infantry battalion, now had four service battalions quartered in it. Needless to say, it was somewhat cramped. " The Seventh " fared no better than the other units in the Brigade in this respect, except that an allotment of " married quarters " was handed over to relieve the pressure of living space. Even this concession left the men crowded, but, after all, in those days it was considerably better than sleeping in the open, and everyone took things as they came and without grumbling.

Almost immediately we got settled down, and began to learn squad drill. Never-ending squad drill all day, and every day. Occasionally the C.O. would give a lecture to relieve the monotony. Three afternoons in the week we went for short marches in the vicinity. During those first two months we underwent all the preliminary stages of the recruit's training, with its concomitant *ennui*. Had it not been for the nucleus of ex-regular W.O.'s and N.C.O.'s, who had been posted to us, it would have been much more difficult to carry on as well as we did. Antiquated, no doubt—as some of them were—they could at any rate instil into the officers and men the main essentials of soldiering. The mainstay of all our training was discipline, and the result was a good foundation of *esprit-de-corps*.

It cannot but amuse those, who can still remember the early days, to look back and picture the strange motley that it presented ; some in mufti ; some in semi-uniform mufti ; a few in khaki—the majority in " Kitchener's blue." One cannot help recalling Sergeant Taylor drilling a squad of recruits in his bowler hat, mufti coat, uniform breeches, and puttees. It almost seemed a matter of personal concern to him whether he or Corporal Dolan could shout the loudest at the " scarified " troops. The laurels would appear to the spectators to be evenly divided on most occasions.

To describe the daily routine in detail during the first few months would be dull for the reader, and for historical purposes of little interest, even to one who participated in it. A general *résumé* of one day will be quite enough to satisfy even the uninitiated.

First parade, 6 a.m. A run round the barrack square ; breakfast, 7-30 a.m. ; 9 a.m. to 12-30 p.m., squad drill and physical training—this parade was held in a field adjoining the barracks ; dinner at 1 p.m., etc. ; 2 p.m., a short route march or an outpost scheme *in the same old field*, then tea ; and probably, three times a week, a lecture in the gymnasium about 6 p.m. Perhaps a night outpost scheme, *in the same old field*, which didn't look quite so bad in the dark, though it was much colder.   Talking of outpost schemes recalls an anecdote worthy of record.   Whilst marching to the training area on a certain evening in November, R.S.M. Kenny was detailed to bring up the rear with a lantern ; this was done in order to avoid the column being run down by a motor car passing us along the road in the dark.   An embryo company commander thought the mere fact of a light being any-where near troops at night was all wrong.   After the exercise was over, he remonstrated with the C.O. about this light, saying, that he thought it " most unrealistic."   The colonel's reply is hardly fit for publication :   " Just what you would think, you b—— fool."

On the 27th November the Brigadier held his first parade inspection of the battalion in the barracks.   Call it an " examina-tion," and perhaps the proceedings will explain themselves more fluently.   Officers were called out in turn to take charge of their respective platoons and put them through their squad drill.   Marvellous to relate, all the officers passed their test. Some were clumsier than others, perhaps, but that was just individual taste.   The G.O.C. dismissed the parade, evidently with satisfaction.   The " examination " in company drill was much more entertaining when it took place, for even the G.O.C. himself seemed a little rusty in this respect.

Having passed out of the stage of elementary drill, an issue of D.P. rifles was the next step in our training career.   Squad drill with arms took the place of squad drill " common or garden," and another mad rush was made to " Infantry Training "—for this was the officers' guide, philosopher and friend in these days. The instructors once again had scope for their rhetoric.   The officers re-formed into a squad of their own, and worked out their own salvation under Major Kenny.   One officer took a long time to fathom the jargon of the instructor :   " When I says ' fix ' you don't fix ; but when I says ' bayonets ' you fix."   (This was a puzzler even to the most keen and intelligent officer.)

So time went on, and by the New Year we became quite pro-ficient in our drill.   March discipline and general smartness showed signs of steady improvement.   Slackness was never allowed to creep in, and never did—the C.O. looked after that. The issue of fifes and drums assisted materially in keeping the men from falling out on long marches, which by now had become more than the five or six miles we had been used to hitherto.

Recruits were now the only thing we lacked.   After the first rush in the late Autumn of 1914 things had gone from bad to worse, and instead of being with " active service " well in view, it seemed further off than ever.   It was most disheartening to all those who had shown such keenness to get on and get out. On the average not more than ten recruits were joining in the

COLONEL R. C. C. COX, Royal Inniskilling Fusiliers.
Commanding Officer, October, 1914—April, 1915

week. This not only deterred training, but made it almost impossible to carry out schemes on a large scale with the few *personnel* at our disposal.

Preliminary instruction in trench digging began early in 1915, but it was not for many months to come that this form of training got anything like the amount of time devoted to it that was necessary for proficiency. On the 11th February Major-General Vesey Dawson, C.V.O., inspected the four battalions of the Brigade in training, and seemed quite pleased with their progress. An amusing and, needless to say, unrehearsed incident occurred during his inspection of " The Seventh." A sham attack had been planned, with various objectives, etc., in the vicinity of Ballyglass. Three companies were detailed to participate in the scheme, and " B " Company were to do company training independently. By the strict instructions of Major Lynch-Blosse, " B " Company were not to appear anywhere in the neighbourhood of the *rendez-vous* for the main scheme.

The Inspecting-General, the C.O. and second-in-command watched the companies attacking from the high ground at the final objective. All went off well until the assault troops were within about 150 yards of the General and his party. Suddenly, from the left flank, there was a yell from a hundred men simultaneously, and through the hedge appeared " B " Company, who, determined not to miss the " show," charged with fixed bayonets, obliquely to the main attack. For a moment the C.O. and second-in-command seemed dumbfounded by this sudden onslaught, but the Major-General was highly delighted, and said, " a most carefully planned flank attack, delivered just in the nick of time." The C.O. said nothing, but probably thought much.

Time passed, and the question of recruits became more and more acute, with the result that, early in March, the G.O.C. 49th Infantry Brigade decided that a party should be sent from the battalion to the regimental district in the north to do a recruiting tour around the country. In accordance with these orders, a party consisting of two officers and about seventy other ranks, including the fife and drum band, were sent up to the depôt. Lieutenant D. H. Morton took command of the party, and was accompanied by Lieutenant A. C. Taggart.

The recruiting party visited Enniskillen, Omagh, Belcoo and many other towns in the counties of Fermanagh and Tyrone, but, on the whole, met with a poor response. The tour came to a close on 27th March, 1915. The battalion was still far from its complete establishment. On the 16th March, 1915, "The Seventh " left the barracks and moved into the hutment camp at Scalaheen. The camp had just been completed, and was

divided into two sections for the accommodation of two battalions.
The 8th Inniskillings took over the camp nearest the barracks,
and the south end was allotted to " The Seventh." Although the
huts were out of the contractor's hands, the camp naturally
needed cleaning up before it became comfortable. At first
the roads were almost impassable with mud, and the parade
ground was little more than a morass. However, assisted by
a spell of fine weather, the men soon put the camp into first-
rate order. The site of the camp, though it was about one mile
west of Tipperary, afforded most excellent opportunities for
training and recreation. The great point was, we were on our
own and could make our own arrangements, which hitherto
had been almost impossible in barracks, owing to the limited
space and accommodation.

Most of the new training area was grazing land, and therefore
there were practically no restrictions as to ground where the troops
could manoeuvre. Company training was carried out independently, and many sham attacks were planned and exercised in
the vicinity of the camp. Many amusing episodes occurred
during these field operations, but one day must stand out vividly
in the memory of those who witnessed the famous " attack "
between " A " and " B " Companies.

The scheme commenced at 9 a.m., and at 9-30 a.m. all objectives
had been taken. Incidentally there was a long discussion on
the road between the company officers as to the exact dispositions
of the troops. At the critical moment the second-in-command
appeared, and watched the progress of events for a few moments.
Unable to bear the sight any longer, he blew his whistle loudly
and stopped the whole proceedings. " I don't know what all
this is about," he said, " but I call it simply h——ish." The
scheme was remodelled and carried out afresh.

During the month many Officers and N.C.O.'s were detailed
to attend courses of instruction in various parts of England
and Ireland. *Personnel* was being gradually selected for the
various special duties in the unit. Transport, machine-gun sections
and signal sections were being formed, if not up to full war
strength, at any rate in proportion to the strength available.
The following Officers and N.C.O.'s were detailed to these various
duties : —

    Lieutenant T. F. Hazell—Transport Officer.
    Sergeant Styles—Transport Sergeant.
    Lieutenant D. H. Morton—Machine-gun Officer.
    Sergeant Hester—N.C.O. Machine-gun.
    Lieutenant W. A. Collis—Signalling Officer.
    Sergeant Kelly—Signal Sergeant.

Special courses were held from time to time in the Command

for " specialists," and the above were detailed to attend these courses when vacancies were allotted to the battalion.

At the beginning of April a preliminary issue of leather equipment was made to the battalion, and in the course of a fortnight all officers and other ranks were fitted out. On the 14th April the Brigadier inspected us in our new equipment. During the inspection the band played selections, and afterwards the General congratulated the C.O. on the smart appearance of the men, and the marked improvement in their drill movements on parade. Company training being now almost at an end, practices were held daily in rifle fire on the miniature range in the camp. These practices were carried out independently by companies under the technical supervision of Lieutenant A. L'E. Brownlow and Sergeant McCluskey, the battalion musketry experts. The keenness evinced by all ranks in these preliminary fire practices was very great. Not only was there great personal competition in the various platoons, but companies vied with one another to gain the highest aggregate score in the battalion.

In the midst of this new era of our training our commanding officer, Colonel R. C. C. Cox, Royal Inniskilling Fusiliers, was posted to another command. The loss of the commanding officer was felt very keenly by all ranks. Since our formation the Colonel had worked indefatigably for our efficiency, and it seemed such bad luck that he should have to leave us, just as we had overcome what one might term the kindergarden stage. It may be a satisfaction to him to know that his efforts were not in vain. By his constant supervision and lectures to the officers and men he infused that sense of discipline, *esprit-de-corps* and comradeship which formed the bed-rock of all our future successes. On April 10th, 1915, he bade the battalion farewell, and the train left Tipperary Station to the strains of " Auld Lang Syne."

A short inter-regnum took place between the departure of Colonel Cox and the arrival of our new C.O., during which period Major Lynch-Blosse automatically assumed command.

On the 17th April Lieutenant-Colonel Michael Hughes assumed command of the battalion. Our new commanding officer commenced his military career in the 3rd Battalion Gordon Highlanders in 1879. In 1883 he was gazetted to the 2nd Life Guards with whom he served until 1896, when he retired. In 1899 he rejoined the army and served throughout the South African War. In this campaign he commanded various detachments and units, amongst others a squadron of cavalry under General French in the advance from Pretoria to Koomatipoort.

The strength of the battalion when Colonel Hughes took over command was approximately 32 officers and 550 other ranks.

.   .   .   .   .   .

On May 1st, the battalion held a most successful smoking concert in the camp. This concert was the first of its kind and afforded an opportunity to the promoters of discovering the talent available. Lieutenants Murray and McCormick, assisted by Privates Joyce, Kenwright and Kerr, formed a nucleus in the entertainment line, and organised many of the most successful " smokers " held in the battalion. Lieutenant E. N. Flook contributed in the form of recitations, which were very popular amongst all ranks.

During the month an effort was made to interest the men in athletic sports. The C.O. decided to establish a representative committee for the purpose of co-ordinating games and sports. As a result of this proposal, Captain R. G. Kerr was elected president. On the 24th May " The Seventh " held their first athletic sports meeting. Amongst other events perhaps the cross-country race was the most attractive and attained the best results. The event was open to the 7th and 8th Battalions, and the following is the detail of the results :—1st, Private McAlevey (7th Battalion) ; 2nd, Corporal Duffey (8th Battalion) ; 3rd, Corporal McGuire (7th Battalion) ; 4th Private Callaghan (7th Battalion) ; 5th, Private Martin (7th Battalion) ; 6th, Lance-Corporal Byrne (8th Battalion) ; 7th, Private Cassidy (8th Battalion) ; 8th, Corporal Shaw (7th Battalion) ; 9th, Private Moore (8th Battalion) ; 10th, Private Banks (7th Battalion).

The C.O. presented ten prizes, and Mrs. Hughes distributed them at the conclusion of the sports.

Training progressed with appreciable rapidity during May. Longer marches were undertaken, and rigid march discipline was observed. Full equipment was carried by both officers and men on all field operations from the beginning of the month. Miniature fire practices had now almost ceased, except for newly-joined recruits. Almost every day companies went to Ballyglass Range to fire their musketry course with ball ammunition. Great competition was shown throughout the Brigade to gain the highest battalion score. At the termination of the course we were informed, to our great satisfaction, that " The Seventh " had topped the list. The most irksome duty connected with the musketry classifications was " butt duty." During the hot weather being cooped up in the butts all day, marking and pasting up the targets after each practice was fired, was most tiring.

Almost coincident with the latter stages of the musketry course, the C.O. received orders to detail 300 other ranks as a draft to reinforce the 10th Division, prior to their departure overseas. Needless to say, at our present strength, this would almost leave us a mere skeleton unit once more. The other battalions

(Photo kindly lent by Major Ross White.)

THE DRAFT ON PARADE, JUNE, 1915—TIPPERARY BARRACKS.

in the Brigade received similar instructions, and on the 11th June the drafts were despatched to join the various units to which they were detailed. A few officers accompanied the parties for draft-conducting duties, and on arrival at Basingstoke handed over their drafts and returned to the Brigade. No one felt the loss of these 300 men more than the commanding officer, who expressed his regret at their departure in the following extract from battalion orders :—" I cannot allow the 300 men " detailed for service to leave my command without putting on " record how much I regret their departure from this regiment. " I feel sure that the draft will never forget that they were trained " in ' The Seventh,' and that the honour and credit of the regiment " are still in their hands to uphold, and by their good conduct set " others an example. I wish them well wherever they may be " sent." To the officers who had served with the battalion since its formation it was most disheartening to lose practically all our *personnel* at a time when they had got to such a state of efficiency. During the first week in June, Captain W. D. Chambers, commanding " A " Company, was transferred to the R.A.M.C.

As a result of the loss of these drafts the higher command appeared to have only two courses open to them, viz.—either to disband the unit altogether or amalgamate it with the 8th Battalion. In point of fact, they adopted neither of these.

The divisional commander, in consultation with the C.O., decided that, should the latter be able to obtain sufficient recruits on his own initiative, and at his own personal expense, the battalion might be reorganised independently, and remain " The Seventh " as hitherto. It is understood that the C.O. agreed, and gave such a guarantee to the G.O.C., with the result that the month of June was devoted almost entirely to organising and collecting men for the battalion. Lieutenant E. Gallagher succeeded in collecting a fair number of recruits from the North of Ireland, and the C.O. himself organised propaganda throughout his estates in England. By these efforts and those of the regimental depôt the battalion raised sufficient men to recommence training.

As a result of our recruiting campaign, the C.O. raised 670 men for the battalion by his own efforts. About 580 of these were recruited in Ireland, and the remainder in the north of England.

Thanks to the combined efforts of the existing W.O.'s. and N.C.O.'s under the supervision of Major Lynch-Blosse, new arrivals were put through the preliminary stages of squad and arms drill. By the end of July we had almost sufficient *personnel* to re-form platoons and companies, under their respective commanders. During the interval, the junior officers underwent a course of instruction in tactics and topography under Major Reid. Operation orders, writing reports, billeting schemes and map reading were the principal subjects dealt with.   The work was most interesting and instructive, and several long-distant schemes were undertaken with remarkably good results.

The course of instruction was somewhat abruptly brought to a close about the 20th July.   The reason for this was caused by a strong rumour that we were about to move for a camp in the South of Ireland.   For the next week the men were practised in pitching tents and learning the duties connected with life under canvas.   Our destination, according to rumour, was to be Bally-hooley Camp, somewhere in the vicinity of the 47th and 48th Brigades, in Co. Cork.   The move was cancelled before the end of the month, and definite instructions came through that the 49th Infantry Brigade would move north at an early date.   The 8th Royal Inniskilling Fusiliers and the 8th Royal Irish Fusiliers were the first units in the Brigade to leave for Ulster.   They left in the last week of July.

On the 2nd August, Lieutenant-Colonel Hughes and the officers gave an " at home " at the camp.   With the approval of the Brigadier, a general holiday was given to the troops, and the battalion held a most successful sports meeting during the afternoon.   The regimental band, drums, and Irish pipers, played selections throughout the day.   It was the first occasion on which the new brass band—presented to the battalion by the C.O.— appeared in public.

Many handsome cups and prizes were distributed to the winners of the various events.   Private J. Campbell captured the battalion challenge cup ;   Private F. Smyth, Corporal McCusker and Sergeant Walsh got many prizes in different events, and Captain R. G. Kerr took the officers' race.   The latter was one of the most amusing events of the afternoon.   The relay race was won by " B " Company, and the tug-of-war (open to the 49th Brigade) went to the 7th Royal Irish Fusiliers.   That the sports were such an all-round success was due to the efforts of the C.O. and the members of the committee who organised the entire arrangements and programme of events.

Early in August instructions were received from the Brigade office that the battalion would move at an early date to Finner Camp, Co. Donegal.   Accordingly, on 5th August, Captain J. Ritty and Lieutenant G. A. C. Walker, with about thirty other ranks, were sent up north as an advance party.   By some mis-adventure they found, on arrival, that no tents were available. This caused a considerable, though unavoidable, delay in the arrival of the main body from Tipperary.   However, in about ten days the arrangements were satisfactorily completed, and on the 19th August the battalion left Tipperary for Finner.   On arrival at

Ballyshannon, where we detrained, the battalion received a hearty welcome in their new station. The inhabitants of the village turned out *en masse* to greet the new arrivals. Flags and other emblems of welcome were displayed throughout the main street as the battalion marched through on their way to camp.

The camp was situated on the high ground, midway between Ballyshannon and Bundoran, and afforded a most excellent position in the summer months. Before we left in the autumn it became very cold, due to its exposure to the wind from every side. Fortunately, the weather was fairly good on the whole and favourable for outdoor training. Our chief objective, however, in this district was to make a final effort for recruits and get the unit up to strength before leaving Ireland permanently.

The G.O.C. of the division visited the battalion early in September, and expressed satisfaction at the general appearance and work of the men. Not only did he inspect the companies and specialists individually, but he also examined with the greatest care the transport and the management of the horse lines.

Nothing extraordinary remains to be recorded regarding the training at Finner Camp. Many recruiting marches were undertaken throughout the district, but the response on the whole was weak and not by any means up to our expectations. At the end of August we got instructions that we were to be sent shortly to England. Undoubtedly, the men had benefited from their stay on the coast. The bracing air, after the relaxing heat of the summer in Tipperary, did much towards making the battalion fit for the great campaign of intensive training which ensued on the "other side."

About the 8th September, 1915, the Brigade left Ireland. "The Seventh" entrained at Ballyshannon en route for Dublin, where they embarked on R.M.S. *Connaught* for Holyhead, and thence proceeded by train to the South of England.

. . . . . .

Before leaving Ireland the commands of the various companies were definitely settled, and it must have been very gratifying to the C.O. to know that the appointments made by him turned out to be more than satisfactory in every respect. The companies were commanded as follows :—

"A" Company—Captain Victor H. Parr.
"B"   ,,   —Captain R. Goodman Kerr.
"C"   ,,   —Major Alexander D. Reid.
"D"   ,,   —*Major Mathew J. Kenny.
                   —Captain C. H. Stainforth.

---

* Major Kenny did not proceed overseas with his company, and Captain C. H. Stainforth took over command.

CHAPTER II.

IN TRAINING (WOKING AND BORDON).

Arriving in England—In training at Woking—Musketry at Bisley Ranges —The death of Sergeant Kelly—Rehearsal inspection parade at Chobham Ridges—The inspection by H.M. the Queen at Aldershot —Lieutenant-General Sir Lawrence Parsons, K.C.B., bids us farewell at Woking—Departure to Bordon (Guadelope Barracks)—Christmas, 1915—Trench instruction—Arrival of new drafts—The last battalion concert—Visit of Father Vaughan—Final arrangements before leaving England — Brigadier-General Douglas Longe, Lieutenant-Colonel Michael Hughes, Major R. Lynch-Blosse and Major M. J. Kenny hand over their commands—Lieutenant-Colonel H. N. Young assumes command of the battalion—Departure for France on the 16th February, 1916.

On the 9th September, after a long and wearisome railway journey from Holyhead, the battalion arrived at the detraining station. It was some distance to our new quarters, and most of us were more than a little tired of the march by the time we arrived at Inkerman Barracks Woking. Properly speaking, the barracks was situated at Knaphill, about two miles outside the town of Woking.

For a few days after our arrival we did little in the way of training, with the exception of the usual daily drill parades. Most of our efforts were directed on making the men comfortable in their new quarters and cleaning up the barracks, which, incidentally, needed it badly. Several kit inspections and equipment-checking parades were held by companies to sum-marise and, if necessary, make good deficiencies which occurred during the move across the Channel. Our accommodation in Woking, even though we were not up to full strength, was, to say the least, decidedly cramped. The 8th Inniskilllings and ourselves shared the billets, which in peace time would only be sufficient for one battalion.

After the first week, our chief centre of activity became the rifle ranges at Bisley. Almost every day two companies were

LIEUT.-COLONEL MICHAEL HUGHES, Commanding Officer April, 1915—February 1916.

detailed for firing practices. Though the work on the ranges was very interesting and instructive, under the guidance of highly efficient musketry experts, yet the unavoidable waiting about at the firing points slackened the enthusiasm of the keenest shots. To add to the monotony of delay in waiting for the various details, the weather was most unpleasantly cold and raw for the time of year. It was not until the end of October that the musketry course was completed, and even then, there were many who joined the battalion in small drafts who had still to go through the course.

Towards the middle of October some batches of trained men were sent to us from Omagh to assist in bringing us up to strength. These parties, for the most part, were more than counterbalanced by the drafts we were obliged to send back to the depôt as unfit for service in the field, and consequently of no further use for our requirements. Many of these were ex-regular army instructors who had retired some years before the outbreak of war, and who had given us invaluable assistance in the preliminary stages of our training.

A sad occurrence happened on the 8th November, by the sudden death of Sergeant J. A. Kelly, D.C.M., the battalion signalling sergeant. The deceased had served for twenty-one years with the " 1st Battalion," in which he had held the position of signal sergeant. His loss was very keenly felt by the battalion, as it was chiefly due to his efforts that the signallers had reached such a state of efficiency.

Certainly, no time was wasted during these days of our intensive training. Rumour had been current for several weeks that it was not improbable that, before the end of December, we should be sent overseas. It seemed impossible, unless we got another two hundred trained men drafted in, that we *could* be sent away as soon as one was led to believe. The officers who had been with the battalion since its formation were very keen to get out, and worked hard to train the latest arrivals up to the standard required. The Quartermaster (Lieutenant W. Reid) had the most unenviable and laborious task of anyone. Overseas equipment and stores were being gradually substituted for those which we had been using for home service only. Specialists' and technical stores were issued, and were used in our field training. Thanks to the efforts of the quartermaster and his staff, the issue of the various items was expedited, and by the beginning of December (with the exception of those articles only issued to those proceeding immediately overseas) we were almost complete. Before the final musketry practices were finished, the Brigadier decided to carry out field operations on the training areas in the vicinity. These operations were carried out almost entirely by day, and generally took place about once a week.   Several billeting schemes and outpost manoeuvres took place in the neighbourhood of Pirbright.   The march discipline and the physical fitness of the men during some of the Brigade schemes carried out at this time showed a most marked improvement.   It was an extremely rare occurrence for a man to fall out on the line of march, though the conditions at times were most tiring and laborious.

On the 19th November, the battalion marched to Chobham Ridges, where the 16th (Irish) Division was concentrated in " review order," to rehearse the forthcoming inspection by Her Majesty Queen Mary.   The parade was carried out under the supervision of Lieutenant-General Sir Archibald Hunter, K.C.B., D.S.O., the G.O.C. of the Aldershot Command.   Accompanied by our Divisional Commander and the generals of his staff, the G.O.C. inspected the various battalions of the division, and he then took the salute as the units " marched past."   Unfortunately, the weather was anything but propitious for the review. Snow lay on the ground, and, like similar functions of its kind, we were kept standing for several hours prior to the inspection. During the forming-up of the different units for the march past many amusing incidents occurred—unintentionally so, of course.   The parade ground was seething with " red tabs," who shouted inaudible and incoherent words of command.   It seemed to be the delight of each brigade staff to try and " drown out " their neighbours.   Somehow or other, order was unravelled from apparent confusion.   From a company commander's point of view, it was always better on these occasions to give a deaf ear to the medley of orders and counter-orders, and to " paddle his own canoe."   The men kept their direction and line with remarkable accuracy in the march past.   Unfortunately, the ground near the spot chosen for the saluting base was anything but level, and the " left wheel in close column " as the companies disengaged was somewhat " ragged," to use the military vernacular.   After the parade the battalion transport met us with the men's dinners, and everyone enjoyed an hour's rest before returning to barracks.   The battalion marched home in the afternoon, and arrived in barracks about 6 o'clock.

For the following fortnight companies were given a thorough exercise in " ceremonial."   Numerous practices were held in the drill field adjoining the barracks in marching past and forming up in review order.   Up to this we had done very little ceremonial drill, and the consequence was that the parades were not altogether perfect.   They were not, however, devoid of a certain amount of humour.   On some occasions the " book " did not agree in detail with the peculiar regimental customs of certain officers, with the result that many discussions took place as to the correct way of doing various movements. After a week the men got well into it, and the officers considered themselves " experts " !

On the 2nd December the great day arrived, and the division was inspected by Her Majesty the Queen at the " Queen's Parade," Aldershot. Unlike the rehearsal a few weeks before, the weather was fine, which made the drill and movement much easier than on the previous occasion. The 49th Infantry Brigade, with ourselves as leading battalion, presented a smart appearance on parade, and marched past in very good line. After the parade the Brigadier congratulated the C.O. on the smart turn-out of the battalion. The march home was the most arduous part of the proceedings, but none of the men were the worse for it. It was nearly 9 p.m. before " The Seventh " got back to Woking.

A few days previous to the " Queen's inspection " we were officially notified that the division was proceeding overseas in the course of the next fortnight, but that it had been decided that the 49th Brigade should remain behind for a short time, and rejoin them later on active service. The reason of this order was, obviously, because we were not yet up to full strength, and that many of our existing *personnel* had but recently joined. Naturally, the 49th Brigade was not therefore in the same state of efficiency as the other two brigades in the division. Needless to say, the disappointment was very great when we were told we were not to go out for another few months, but by this time we had become accustomed to the lack of Other Ranks, and the best course was to suffer patiently.

The Divisional Commander (Sir Lawrence Parsons, K.C.B.) told us in his farewell speech that he was not accompanying the division to France. Before laying down his office, he said that he wished to express his satisfaction, not only at the smart appearance of the men, but also on their good behaviour during their stay at Woking. He informed us that we were moving to Bordon in a few days, and he hoped that it would not be long before we should rejoin the remainder of the division, " somewhere in France." After the parade the G.O.C. shook hands with the officers and wished them the best of good luck. Three cheers were given for the General as he left the parade ground.

On the 4th December, 1915, the 49th Infantry Brigade moved by route march to Bordon, a training area about ten miles southwest of Aldershot.

The battalion made an early start, and, despite the shocking state of the roads and the downpour of rain, arrived at Guadelope Barracks none the worse for the long march. As usual, we shared billets with the 8th Inniskillings, but on this occasion we got the lion's share. For a time, at any rate, the accommodation was sufficient for both units, but later on, when our final drafts arrived, it was only with great difficulty and crowding that we could manage to get everybody in.   Most of our part of the camp was composed of married quarters, which meant many extra fatigues for keeping billets clean.

There was no time in our new area to concentrate on comforts in billets, or accommodation—-it was a period of intensive training for all.   Tremendous activity and enthusiasm infused the whole brigade in their anxiety to follow the rest of the division to France.   With the exception of the Christmas festivities (which, by the way, lasted a week), the battalion was on the go all day and every day.

All our efforts were directed on field training and trench duties.   Peculiar as it may seem, we had up to this had very little instruction in trench life, and the established routine of " manning and relieving."   True, we had many lectures about the life and routine of stationary warfare in France, but we needed some practical work in this branch to appreciate it thoroughly.   This was all put into execution during our stay at Bordon.   At least twice a week, companies would be detailed to dig, and improve the model trenches on the training area in the Hogmoor enclosure.   By the end of December quite a fair system of trenches and redoubts had been completed, and it became part of the weekly programme to hold an all-night scheme in the vicinity.   As a general rule these operations took the form of inter-company trench reliefs, and during the few hours that companies held the front line the men were kept busy widening and improving the defences generally.   On these occasions telephonic and other means of communication were established between the various headquarters.   Battalion Headquarters was situated in a suitable spot about four hundred yards behind the front line, and the C.O. and his adjutant sat down for the night on the roadside to await messages and give instructions to the companies.   On occasions the Brigadier would walk round the area supervising the work.   The Brigade Major (Major Rudkin) was always in evidence, pointing out new work to be done and explaining difficulties which continually cropped up.   Within a few weeks of our arrival at Bordon, Christmas was round once again—our second Christmas at home.

Although the camp was in such an out-of-the-way spot, we managed to enjoy ourselves very thoroughly for a few days. Thanks to the efforts of the C.O. and Captain Kerr, a most successful smoking concert was held for the men on Christmas Eve in the theatre.   Besides the local talent procured within the battalion and the other units of the brigade, some professional artistes from the " Three Arts Club " in London came

" A " Company—Bordon, 1916.

down to assist us, and altogether the evening was most entertaining, and highly appreciated by everybody. The Brigadier,
Mrs. Longe and many officers and their families within the
area visited us that evening, and they all seemed pleased with
the " show." At the conclusion of the concert, the promoters
were given a rousing welcome, and the C.O. made a short speech,
in which he thanked the helpers, and wished them, and the
audience, a happy Christmas.

Christmas Day was celebrated in the usual way. The C.O.,
the adjutant and officers of the battalion visited the men at
dinner time, and wished them all success in the coming year.
Customary toasts were proposed, amidst much cheering.

On Boxing Day the 7th played the 8th Battalion at football,
and the former won a keenly contested game by four goals to two.

It was not until the New Year arrived that we settled down to
work in earnest again. On the last night of 1915, the officers'
mess invited their friends to a guest night, and by midnight
the subalterns got together and took over the fife and drum band
to welcome in 1916 ! The incident caused much amusement
in the camp, but the attempts at the " Sprig-of-Shillelagh " were
not exactly pleasing to one with a musical ear.

The first week in January saw us well at it again—on intensive
training operations. Throughout the month, representatives from
the staff of the Aldershot Command paid us frequent visits of
inspection during our field work. Certainly, the surrounding
country was ideal for the requirements of the brigade, and full
advantage was taken to exercise the troops. Space will not allow
some of the details to be recorded, but it may be taken as a fact,
that not a few of us got lost on many occasions. For the platoon
officer it was often a wise precaution to keep out of harm's way,
though it was not always as easy to manoeuvre as one might
imagine. At the end of a day's training nobody was " missing,"
and the best part of the scheme was hearing the various opinions
afterwards—one never heard what " the men " had to say on the
subject, though it was not difficult to guess ! " Yesterday," however, was forgotten with the arrival of " to-morrow." There
could be no better motto for us than "Sufficient unto the day was
the evil thereof," and some such evil days (had we known it then)
were drawing nearer and nearer.

About the middle of January several drafts of fully-trained
men joined the battalion ; some of these men were transferred
from English and Scottish regiments, and a few were re-posted
from other regiments at the depôt. The inclusion of these
other ranks brought our strength up considerably, and, coupled
with the few men who had joined recently from our own depôt,
we were now nearly nine hundred strong.

B

Shortly after the arrival of these drafts the Brigadier inspected
the battalion in full marching order—and, incidentally, for
the last time during his command of the brigade.

On the evening of the 23rd January, Father Bernard Vaughan,
accompanied by Lieutenant-General Sir Lawrence Parsons,
K.C.B., gave a lecture to the brigade in the theatre. The hall
was packed so tightly that one could scarcely see a gap between
the faces. The lecturer, in the course of a most eloquent and
humorous speech, expressed the hope that all ranks, whoever
they might be, and to whatever unit of the brigade they might
happen to belong, would keep one great ideal before them,
wherever they were sent to, and that was—" to be the best man,
of the best battalion, of the best brigade, of the finest division
in the British Army. With such a spirit of *esprit-de-corps*," he
said, " you must do well."

At the conclusion of his discourse he gave his Benediction to
the troops.

Before passing to the last stage of all, and that final fortnight
of our training and activity before proceeding overseas, we must
recall the last smoking concert in the theatre, organised and so
well carried out on the initiative of Lady Lynch-Blosse, with
the approval of the C.O. The concert was held for the benefit
of a comforts fund for " The Seventh," when they had left for
active service. It would be impossible to over-estimate the debt
of gratitude we owe to Lady Lynch-Blosse and the many friends
who assisted, supported and subscribed to the fund. The comforts, which were subsequently sent out to France, were greatly
appreciated by us all, and it may be a satisfaction to the donors
to know how welcome their gifts were.

Referring for a moment to the entertainment itself—it only
remains to be said that it was a most successful evening, and
greatly enjoyed by all. The C.O. gave a short address after
the concert, in which he thanked those who had taken so much
trouble with the organisation, and wished the scheme the
best of good luck. The officers entertained many of the artistes
and their friends to a small dance afterwards in the mess, which
was the *finale* to a very enjoyable evening. By the end of January
it was semi-official that we were " booked " for France within
the next fortnight, though no definite orders were received as
to the probable date of embarkation.

Most of the time during the first week of February was taken up
in getting the men medically inspected, vaccinated if necessary,
and inoculated   Everything was rushed in at the last moment,
even to the anti-gas practices. It almost seems laughable now
to think of that first anti-gas drill on the battalion parade ground.
Two P.H. helmets were issued to the men, and a few minutes

"C" Company—Bordon, 1916.

were spent in trying them on. Little we knew how soon we would have to test them in reality, and at what a cost !

On the 7th February we lost our brigade commander, Brigadier-General R. Douglas Longe. According to instructions received through the Aldershot Command, no senior officers were permitted to proceed overseas over a certain age limit. This order affected many officers in the brigade and in our own battalion. The C.O. (Lieutenant-Colonel Michael Hughes), Major R. Lynch-Blosse, our second-in-command, and Major M. J. Kenny, commanding " D " Company, all came under this category. Needless to say, we were sorry to lose our best friends, but no more so than they were to leave us. It was with the deepest regret that we afterwards read of the death of General Longe ; he was the founder of the brigade, and had watched us with personal pride and care through the long months of training, until we had become, at any rate, what was in our opinion, the best brigade in the New Army. Undoubtedly, there were many who thought the same before us, and after, but it did nobody any harm, especially ourselves—it inspired confidence.

On the 12th February we had our first brigade scheme under the eye of the new brigadier—Brigadier-General Leveson-Gower. It was the usual trench manning and relieving operation on the training area near Hogmoor Enclosure. At the time nobody seemed to regret that it was the last time we should see those trenches, which had become so familiar during the last two months in Bordon.

On the 14th February the battalion was taken over by Lieutenant-Colonel H. N. Young, Royal Inniskilling Fusiliers, and for the next few days mobilisation proceeded. Packing and weighing kits, issuing active service requirements, and handing in superfluous kit to store, were the order of the day, until the time came for our final parade and the march-off.

About 2 p.m. on the 16th February, we paraded on the road outside the barracks and marched to the station, where we entrained for Southampton.

Lieutenant-Colonel Michael Hughes, Major Lynch-Blosse and several of the officers' relations bade us farewell and good luck as we pulled out of the station, bound for our new life, and our real part in the Great War.

Of necessity, several officers and N.C.O.'s remained behind in charge of details. Most of these rejoined us later in France. Lieutenant T. F. Hazell was transferred to the Royal Flying Corps a few days after our departure. In this service he distinguished himself in the field in a most exceptional way, and won many distinctions.

     *   *   *   *   *   *

To the uninitiated, or to those who were not serving in the battalion in those days at Tipperary, Ballyshannon, Woking and Bordon, it would be difficult, if not well-nigh impossible, to follow the smaller details of our life from this short *précis*. It is, however, the general outline of those incidents which have been related that will recall to many their own individual and personal contact with their early days of soldiering; to the others, I hope the narrative will form a suitable introduction to the records of our fuller and more strenuous life with the vast armies in France. It would be invidious of me—a mere junior officer in the battalion—to compare, or in any way criticise the merits of the senior officers who did not proceed overseas with us. It should be sufficient gratification to them to know that their organisation and well-directed instruction bore its fruit in our future service in the field. The spirit of comradeship, and devotion to duty they had fostered at home never left the battalion, even in its hardest trials. And what more coveted title could the unit gain for itself, and the regiment of which we were so proud to belong to, than " The Fighting Seventh."

PART II.

—◦—

INTRODUCTION

BY

MAJOR-GENERAL SIR W. B. HICKIE, K.C.B.

Late G.O.C. 16th (IRISH) Division

η ταύταν η̃ ἐπὶ ταύτας

Plutarch

Loos Salient
Hulluch, April 27th, 1916
The Somme, 1916
Wytschaete, 1917
Ypres, 1917

INTRODUCTION
Part II.

In the dedication of this history the writer has quoted the motto which was adopted by the Division after its share in the Battle of the Somme in 1916.

No Division in France could have upheld that motto more worthily than did the Irish Division, from March, 1916, when it first took its place in the line at Loos up to the overwhelming disaster of Epehy and Roncoy in March, 1918. The story of the 7th Royal Inniskilling Fusiliers up to the date of the amalgamation with the 8th Battalion, is the history of the Division. Through those two years they took part in every venture. The discipline, the valour, the tradition and the spirit of the Inniskilling Fusiliers were with them always. Therefore they achieved success ; therefore they won the admiration and the gratitude of all those with whom they served ; and therefore I, their old Divisional Commander, can say of the Battalion and its gallant Colonel—" Everywhere and always faithful."

W. B. HICKIE.
Major-General,
Late G.O.C. 16th (Irish) Division.

Slevoyre,
  Borrisokane,
    Co. Tipperary,
      September, 1920.

CHAPTER III.

THE LOOS SALIENT—FEBRUARY to MAY 31st, 1916.

Leaving Bordon—Embarkation at Southampton and arrival in France
—Berguette—The march to Nédonchelle—Move to L'Ecleme—
Philosophe West and first impressions of the line—Instruction under
46th Infantry Brigade—Philosophe East and the formation of the
battalion cemetery—The march to Cauchy-à-La-Tour |via Vaudricourt
—Major Brooke assumes command—The bombardment of April
6th—Noeux-les-Mines and the inspection of " B " Company by the
Army Commander—Events leading up to the gas attack at Hulluch
—The affairs of April 27th and 29th—The Brigade Commander's
inspection on May 3rd—Congratulations from the Army and Divisional
Commanders *re* operations—Noeux-les-Mines and " rest "—Training in
Divisional Reserve—The practice raid on May 9th—Loos—Formation
of Major Reid's special company—Relief by the Berks Regiment,
May 29/30—Major Reid gives a typical picture of a Company
Commander's life in the trenches, entitled " A Point of View."

On the 16th February, 1916, shortly after 1 p.m., the battalion
entrained at Bordon Station, en route for Southampton Docks.
Lieutenant-Colonel Michael Hughes and Major Lynch-Blosse bade
us farewell and good luck as the train pulled out.   Southampton
was reached by 4-30 p.m., and the battalion, which was met by
the guides of the A.M.L.O., marched to the docks and
embarked within an hour and a half on the s.s. *Mona Queen*,
a paddle steamer with very limited accommodation.

The battalion transport, baggage and quartermaster's staff
embarked on a special steamer from the docks and rejoined us
later on arrival in France.

Orders were received, shortly after our embarkation, that the
time of our departure was uncertain, but it was definite that the
boat would not sail, at any rate, before morning. The C.O. was
granted permission to disembark the battalion on the wharf early
the following morning, and he took the opportunity of inspecting
us for the first time, since he had taken over command, and of
afterwards giving a short address.   In the course of a few words
our C.O. summed up the duties of a soldier on active service, and
what he would expect of the battalion.   " Orders must be obeyed

promptly," he said, "and without hesitation. You must for ever strive to keep up the traditions of your regiment and become a fighting unit second to none."

At 4 o'clock, the same afternoon, our boat got under way and we sailed slowly down the Solent, to the strains of the "Sprig-of-Shillelagh," played by the battalion pipers. Accompanied by two destroyers we crossed the Channel. It was a wretched and truly miserable night. Rain came down in buckets, and the wind blew unmercifully from the south-west. Our little paddle steamer dived, pitched, and rolled all night, and more than 70 per cent. of the *personnel* suffered badly from *mal-de-mer*.

Shortly after 2 o'clock the following morning, we arrived at Le Havre, but the troops were not allowed to disembark until just after 6 o'clock. Fortunately, we had no transport or baggage to look after, except personal equipment, so it was but a matter of twenty minutes to disembark the battalion and form up on the quay. We marched about two miles to the rest camp, and had some breakfast under the most unfavourable weather conditions. Some of the officers were granted the privilege of being allowed into town for a few hours where they had *déjeuner*.

That evening we were initiated into that mysterious and depressing mode of travelling known as "the French troop train." By 9 o'clock the battalion arrived at the station, and entrained for an unknown destination. With the exception of one very dilapidated first-class carriage, labelled "officers," a few open trucks for the limbered wagons and miscellaneous vehicles, the train was composed of covered-in cattle trucks labelled in chalk—40 *Hommes*, 10 *Chevaux*—nobody seemed to object if you cared to mix them. At 10-30 o'clock the train pulled out of Havre, and judging by our ultimate time record it must have toured most of France during the night. Sometimes we would jog along at 20 m.p.h. for several hours, then for the next hour the train seemed to crawl, shunt, stop and start alternately. During rather a longer halt than usual outside Calais (Les Fontinettes), our mascot "Tip" jumped off the train and was never seen again. A stop at St. Omer gave us an opportunity for a wash, of which we felt badly in need. By 7 p.m. we arrived at Berguette Station (about five miles north of Lillers), and here we detrained and made tea before starting out for billets.

The Brigade Staff-Captain (Major Ross White) met the battalion on arrival, informing us that our destination was Nédonchelle, about nine miles march from the station. Major A. D. Reid and Lieutenant G. A. C. Walker were detailed by the C.O. to accompany the staff-captain in his car to the village, and make arrangements for billeting the men and alloting them quarters before their arrival.   The inhabitants of this pleasant village received us in a most friendly and benevolent manner, which added greatly to our comfort.

The battalion arrived in billets about midnight, with the exception of " A " Company, who remained behind at the station to unload the baggage ; " A " Company arrived at 4 a.m.   Thirty-two officers (including the medical officer, Captain G. O. F. Alley) and 995 other ranks was the total strength of the unit on arrival in France. So far the only casualty had been the mascot " Tip."

Life in billets might have been very pleasant had it not been for the extreme bitterness of the cold and wintry weather. Snow lay half a foot deep over the country the following morning, and during the night the thermometer registered 25 degrees. The state of the roads made training almost out of the question, and most of the time was spent in giving the men lectures and reading the " standing orders " regarding the duties and restrictions of a soldier's life on active service.   The C.O. gave special instructions and was most particular about the mounting of guards, the general smartness of the men in billets, the correct method of saluting, and the exchange of compliments.

On the 20th inst. Major Ross White arrived and took over the duties of second-in-command of the battalion.

On the morning of the 22nd, Major-General Sir W. B. Hickie, K.C.B. (our Divisional Commander), inspected the battalion in a field on the outskirts of the village.   The battalion was drawn up in " quarter column," with the machine-gunners, signallers and pioneers, to a flank. The Divisional Commander expressed his satisfaction at our smart appearance on parade, and owing to the inclemency of the weather gave permission for companies to march off independently after he inspected them. The G.O.C. afterwards lectured the officers in the local schoolhouse, explaining to them the importance of working out and sticking to a plan of operations, and so be always prepared to meet any situation that might arise.

On the 25th we marched to L'Ecleme, about six miles north-west of Bethune. The march was a disagreeable one, owing to the almost glassy state of the roads with frozen snow.   A thaw set in during the afternoon, which made matters easier.   Unlike our last billets, L'Ecleme was an unusual type of village, better described, perhaps, as an area. It was a long and straggling group of farm-houses. "A" Company, on the western edge, were at least a mile from Battalion Headquarters.   Difficulties arose regarding communications in case of a sudden order to move ; this was obviated on the following day by the erection of telephone circuits to the companies. Though still in the Army Reserve area, the sound of the guns was now quite audible, and at night much interest

THE OFFICERS 7TH ROYAL INNISKILLING FUSILIERS—BORDON, FEBRUARY, 1916.

THIRD ROW (*Standing*)—Lieut. E. Gallagher, Lieut. H. B. O. Mitchell, 2/Lieut. J. Cunningham, 2/Lieut. J. Cunningham, 2/Lieut. F. S. Carroll, 2/Lieut. F. A. W. Milligan, Lieut. R. T. Sutton, Lieut. E. N. Flook, Lieut. C. Le Fèvre, Lieut. E. J. McCormick, 2/Lieut. J. Colien, Lieut. R. N. Murray, Capt. Bretherton (Warwicks Regt.) (attached).

SECOND ROW (*Standing*)—2/Lieut. H.W. Ruddock, Lieut. T. Olphert, Lieut. D. H. Morton, Lieut. T. F. Hazell, Lieut. G. A. C. Walker, 2/Lieut. A. E. C. Trimble, 2/Lieut. M. J. Daly, Lieut.-Colonel H. N. Young, Capt. G. O. F. Alley, R.A.M.C; 2/Lieut. H. F. Reid, Lieut. A. L'E. Brownlow, 2/Lieut. G. F. Henderson, 2/Lieut F. J. Kenny, 2/Lieut. H. P. McKenna.

was evinced by the appearance of the flares and star shells on the sky line, in the direction of Neuve Chapelle, Festubert and La Bassée.

During our stay in the village some of our N.C.O.'s and men who were not fit for the strain of trench warfare and exposure, were sent away to the base for employment on the lines of communication.

On the 2nd March we left L'Ecleme for Philosophe West—the final stage towards the line—the crowning period of instruction and training—the game of war in reality.

By a stroke of good luck the weather was fine, almost mild. Our route lay through Gonnehem—Chocques—Béthune, thence straight along the Lens road to Philosophe. We arrived at 4 p.m., and were met by the guides of the 46th Infantry Brigade, to whom we were to be attached for our trench instruction. It was getting late as we marched in, and all that one could see of the village was the two long straight rows of deserted houses on either side of the main road ; at the top of a hill, about 600 yards further on, loomed up Fosse 3, and the slag heaps above the mine shaft. The houses, needless to say, were uninhabited, except by soldiers— this, we were informed, was the reserve position of the brigade holding the front line. The houses at first sight looked in good repair and to be unaffected by hostile shelling, but closer examination showed they had received some attention from the Hun. Perhaps the worst fault to be found with them was the dirt and the lack of windows, which made them so uncomfortable in this wintry weather. No hostile artillery was noticeable during the evening, though our guns fired spasmodically from various positions in the vicinity ; a particularly noisy 6-inch howitzer battery shook the houses as it kept up a slow and regular rate of fire. By 10 p.m. they were silent, and but for the rattling of the limbered wagons on the *pavé* road without, we might have imagined ourselves miles behind the line.

The following morning was spent in inspecting the men before proceeding to the line in the evening—gas helmets, field dressings, rifles, ammunition and other numerous details. By nightfall the battalion had moved into the line by companies in the following detail :—

" A " Coy. (Capt. V. H. Parr) attached to 10th ⎫
    Scottish Rifles. ⎪
" B " Coy. (Capt. J. Ritty) attached to 12th ⎪
    H.L.I. ⎬ 46th Infy. Bde.
" C " Coy. (Major A. D. Reid) attached to 8th ⎪ 15th (Scottish)
    K.O.S.B. ⎪ Division.
" D " Coy. (Capt. C. H. Stainforth) attached ⎪
    to 7th K.O.S.B. ⎭

Battalion Headquarters and its staff moved to Philosophe East—a continuation of our present area, but further east towards Loos—and took over the bakery, still inhabited and carried on by an elderly and rather suspicious-looking Frenchman. Although nearer the line, and within direct observation of enemy artillery, this part of Philosophe was much preferable to the western end, both for accommodation and cleanliness.

The companies remained under the instruction of the Scottish battalions for the next fortnight, during which time the C.O. and adjutant paid frequent visits to the line on tours of inspection and reconnaissance. The hardships and privations suffered by our men during their initiation to trench warfare were most severe—snow and frost reigned alternately, and the unaccustomed exposure brought its toll of sickness and trench feet. Fortunately, the list of casualties from enemy action was comparatively small, in proportion to our wide distribution. Eight fatal casualties resulted in the fourteen days—13419, Sergeant W. T. Mulholland ("D" Company) was the first to succumb to his wounds in the battalion, and by order of the C.O. he was buried in a field at the back of the bakery. This field became the site of the battalion cemetery whilst we were in the Loos Salient, and whenever it was physically possible, all ranks "killed in action" were interred in it. In a few isolated cases some of the dead were buried nearer the line. Such cases were inevitable and beyond our control.

On the 15th March the companies were relieved by various units of the 46th Infantry Brigade, and returned to Philosophe East for rest, and reorganisation as a battalion. The instruction afforded us by the Scotsmen was exceptionally well directed, and we take this opportunity of showing our appreciation.

A word of explanation at this point regarding the order of battle at the time on the army front in general, and a general outline of their dispositions and respective commands will help the reader to grasp the general situation with more freedom, and obviate unnecessary explanations during accounts of future operations in the Loos Salient. We were attached to the centre corps (1st) of the First Army, commanded by General Sir Charles Monro. The 1st Corps was commanded by Lieutenant-General C. T. M'M. Cavanagh, and roughly held from the Hohenzollern Redoubt (south of the La Bassee Canal) to Merok (inclusive).

The order of battle on the 1st of March, 1916, with subsequent reliefs in proportion to trench duty, up till the preparations for the Somme offensive, was as follows :—

1st Division (right)—15th Division (centre)—12th Division (left) and 16th (Irish) Division in reserve. These dispositions were interchangeable monthly.

On St. Patrick's Day the battalion occupied the left sub-sector of the Loos Sector, under the command of the 46th Infantry Brigade, and after two days' instruction as a complete unit was relieved by the 11th A. and S. H. on the night of the 19th-20th.

Captain R. G. Kerr, commanding " B " Company, rejoined the battalion on the 18th, and took over command of his company again. (This officer had remained at Bordon sick, when we left for France.)

On the 20th inst. the battalion moved by road to Vaudricourt, via Mazingarbe and Noeux-les-Mines, and rejoined the divisional command at Cauchy-à-La-Tour on the following day. Vaudricourt possessed probably the best accommodation for billets we ever had the good fortune to meet with in France—unluckily we spent only one night there, as we set off again early the following morning. All the officers, and a fair proportion of the men, were billeted in the château. The château, though it was unoccupied, was exactly as it had been in peace time ; furnished drawing-rooms and salons downstairs, upstairs countless bedrooms—all unspoilt and, so far, immune from the hand of war.

We arrived at Cauchy-à-La-Tour shortly after midday (on the 21st), and were comfortably billeted there for the next ten days. After the cold and mud of the trenches there was many a man who realised, perhaps for the first time in his life, what it was to have a comfortable billet, even though it was only a barn, or the back room of a French farm-house.

The chief attraction of this little village lay in the number of " estaminets." It is true they were forbidden to sell spirits to the troops, but judging from results on pay day it was a matter for consideration whether the proprietors obeyed the law as carefully as they might. " Bier " (very highly watered) and cheap " Vin blanc and Vin rouge " (tasting strongly of vinegar) were their advertised wares. The C.O. dealt strongly with any cases of insobriety, and so the men rarely transgressed.

Training was kept up in billets, but not intensively. After lunch time, the men were left more or less to their own devices, writing letters, playing football, or practising their French on the local inhabitants ; the latter form of recreation caused much amusement and *bonhomie* to everyone. It was not long before the men got quite enough working knowledge of the language to carry on a conversation with " Madame " to get whatever they required. Sometimes Madame would offer her particular pets " du cafe " and sit for hours talking to the men, laughing, gesticulating and speaking French and English alternately. If asked a favour while she was busy, and unable to answer the multifarious questions put to her by the soldiers, she would reply excitedly—*Pas du tout. Pas du tout. C'est bon pour les troupes, mais pas bon pour madame.*

The C.O. spent most of his time in the orderly room, with Captain Taggart and the orderly-room staff, writing orders, answering official letters, plotting defence schemes, interviewing company commanders and other officers to discuss the general welfare of the men.   The paper campaign was incessant, whether in the line or out.   Certificates were rendered by company commanders daily on almost every subject imaginable—socks, rations, pay, equipment, instruction, health, and tactics were made the subject of correspondence through the usual channels.

On the 27th March, the battalion marched out of billets back to the line, this time as a unit of our own division.   We marched to Lapugnoy, and there entrained for Noeux-les-Mines ; we arrived about 9-30 a.m.

An amusing incident worthy of record occurred during our march to the entraining station.   The signal officer, who marched at the head of the battalion, was responsible, when the C.O. was not present, for keeping the correct route.   At the starting point the Colonel was in front, but having rather a fast-walking horse he drew ahead of the battalion by some 400 yards. On reaching Auchel he rode straight through the town, instead of turning off to the right on the outskirts of the town.   The battalion took the Bruay road, and for quite an hour lost the C.O. altogether. Evidently, he must have waited for the battalion at some point on the road, and finding we were not following him he galloped after us, overtaking us near Bruay.   The adjutant and the signal officer were made the butts of very violent language for their mistake !   The matter was considered " closed " on a more careful study of the map.

On the 30th March the commanding officer was granted fourteen days' leave to England for medical reasons, and Major G. F. Brooke (Connaught Rangers) assumed command of the battalion during his absence.   On All Fools' Day (1st April) the battalion relieved the 7th Leinsters in the " Puits 14 bis Sector "—so called on account of a sugar refinery of that name, which was in the enemy's line directly opposite our trenches.   The sector was divided into two sub-sectors, of which this battalion had taken over the left, and had for its boundaries Posen Alley on the north, and Chalk Pit Alley on the south.

" A," " B " and " C " Companies occupied the front line, with " D " Company in the reserve trench, off Gun Alley.

The enemy had superiority of visibility in this sector, due to the natural advantage of having the high ground in his possession, not only from Bois Hugo, but more effectively from Hill 63 to a flank.   The first few days were unattended with any unusual activity on the part of the enemy, excepting the usual " morning hate " and registration, which was mostly directed against the

village of Loos, about half a mile on our right.   Such sudden
bursts of shell fire caused little discomfiture to the garrison of
Loos, as we ourselves experienced later, because they were
invariably directed on certain points which, needless to say, were
unfrequented in daylight.   13410, C.S.M. Taylor (" A " Company)
was killed by a rifle grenade on the 5th inst. whilst on duty in the
front line ; he was a great loss to his company.

Undisturbed as were the first few days of April, comparatively speaking, the 6th of the month brought with it a
most unprecedented bombardment on our trenches.   " B "
Company (Captain R. G. Kerr) was the objective of the severest
gun fire.   Shortly after 1-30 p.m.—in fact, just as the men were
eating their dinners—the bombardment opened.   Captain R. G.
Kerr and the officers were having lunch in their company headquarters when the first shell burst within a few yards of the door,
followed in quick succession by several more.   The officers
quickly got up, followed by the mess servants and batmen, and
tried to get out to the trench.   Before the officers got to the
trench a 5.9 registered a direct hit on the dug-out, and it collapsed.
The officers were fortunate to escape unhurt, but two batmen were
severely wounded, and four signallers were buried in the *debris*,
and, despite the efforts of a continuous working party for the next
twenty-four hours, their bodies were never recovered.   Within
ten minutes of the opening of this artillery onslaught, the enemy
concentrated all his fire on " B " Company's support line.   Salvo
after salvo burst on, or near the trench, with most terrifying rapidity.
For two hours the enemy kept up the demolition of our defences
and then ceased, but not before he had suffered heavily from our
artillery.   This was the first occasion we had observed in which
our guns were not stinted with ammunition.   The courage and
devotion to duty shewn by the men during this terrible ordeal
was beyond praise, and was recognised, as we shall see later, by
the Army Commander.   About twenty casualties was the result
of the shoot, the object of which was never quite understood, as
no infantry action followed, unless it was in retaliation for our
light trench mortar activity.

Another unpleasant incident, but happily not attended with
any serious consequences, was the organised shoot by the enemy
on our Battalion Headquarters.   It was the custom to have sent
up daily a basket containing two pigeons, as an alternate means
of communication to the rear, should all other means fail.   These
birds were kept in the battalion signal office for twenty-four
hours and then released with a practice message if not required
tactically.   During one afternoon they were released, in clear
visibility, within a few yards of the headquarters, and evidently
within the observation of the Boche.   Next morning he " strafed "

the neighbourhood for half-an-hour with " heavy stuff," but his range, though at times uncomfortably accurate, was not correct, and, save for some local damage to the trenches, he caused no casualties.   The incident was one which is worth recording, as it was through all these and countless other details that we gained that great essential " experience," which nothing can supplant, and which can only be gained by the analysis of the thousand-and-one things which happen, or don't happen, daily.

The 8th Royal Inniskilling Fusiliers relieved the battalion on the night of the 6th-7th April, and we moved into Brigade reserve at Philosophe East, where we remained until the 9th inst., and then relieved the 8th Royal Irish Fusiliers in 10th Avenue (Brigade support).   The battalion in Brigade support was generally looked on as having a " cushy job " compared with those in the front system.   The fatigues were wearisome and continuous, but they were chiefly done under cover of darkness.   Hostile activity was very seldom directed on 10th Avenue, excepting, of course, when the enemy contemplated a raid or a local attack ; on such occasions he would shell the trench, but never with any great degree of accuracy, chiefly due to the fact that direct observation from the ground was not easy, as the trench was, for the most part, on the reverse slope.

The dispositions of the battalion in Brigade support were the garrison of 10th Avenue (the old German front line before the Battle of Loos in September, 1915), including the various redoubts according to the sector occupied—Northern Sap Redoubt, Lone Tree Redoubt, 65-Metre Point Redoubt and numerous others unnamed.   One company of the battalion took over the garrison of Gun Trench, a position of close support to the forward system. The greatest drawback to 10th Avenue was the abundance of rats which it harboured.   After dusk the trench was alive with these vermin in all shapes, sizes and colours.   Dug-outs swarmed with the pestilence, and great supervision had to be preserved over the rations, or they would often disappear with alarming rapidity.

On the 11th April, Colonel H. N. Young returned from England and took over command of the battalion once again.   The same night we were relieved by the 8th Munsters, and went back to Mazingarbe for eight days in Divisional reserve.   During the tour in reserve, "B" Company (Captain R. G. Kerr), who had been subjected to the enemy bombardment of April 6th, were inspected and congratulated by the G.O.C. 49th Infantry Brigade on their coolness and courage.   The Brigadier presented the following with the " Parchment of the Irish Division " as a reward for their special good work :—Captain R. G. Kerr, Captain J. Ritty, Lieutenant E. N. Flook, Second-Lieutenant A. E. C. Trimble, Sergeant Brennan and Private Brown.   A further, and unusual, honour for a company was bestowed on " B " Company on the 18th April, with an inspection, followed by a short address, by the Army Commander, General Sir Charles Monro. The inspection took place in the Market Square at Noeux-les-Mines, and was attended by the Battalion, Brigade, Division and Corps Commanders. The G.O.C. First Army shook hands with the officers and N.C.O's. named above, and expressed his great satisfaction with the appearance and smartness of the company on parade. He expressed a hope that the company would live up to the reputation they had earned, and would get their own back on the enemy with interest at no distant date.

On the 20th, the battalion moved up to Philosophe West, and after the usual four days in Brigade reserve moved up to the front line again, this time to a new sub-sector—Hulluch. Relief was carried out in daylight, and was completed by 2-30 p.m. on the 24th. Our new sector extended from Posen Alley on the right up to Holly Lane, and the dispositions from left to right were— " C " Company (Major A. D. Reid), " B " Company (Captain R. G. Kerr), and " A " Company (Captain V. H. Parr) in the front line, with " D " Company (Captain C. H. Stainforth) in the reserve trench, from Vendin Alley on the left to the junction of Posen Alley. Battalion Headquarters was in Curzon Street. Left flank battalion, the 8th Royal Irish Fusiliers. Right flank battalion, the 8th Royal Dublin Fusiliers. (The front held by the battalion was 1,000 yards approximately.) The relief, although carried out under most perfect weather conditions and ideal visibility, was not hampered in any way by enemy action ; in fact, quite the reverse of what one would have expected from future developments, the line was strangely silent—uncannily so.

On the 26th April hostile artillery activity increased in a most marked degree. Vendin Alley, Posen Alley, Pont Street and other " communicaters " were intermittently fired on during the day with 4.2's and 5.9's. Special attention was directed against gunner O.P.'s., which resulted in some cases in their total destruction. Extensive damage was done to the trenches in the vicinity of Curzon Street during the afternoon—in fact, the enemy's action was a strong indication of a final registration preparatory to a raid or a local attack. A significant report was received from Brigade Headquarters the same evening, in which the G.O.C. emphasised, in view of the important information which had been given by a German deserter (a copy of which he enclosed), the urgent necessity for organising wiring parties at night to construct a formidable defence against surprise. In addition to the strengthening and maintenance of the existing wire entanglements, he ordered that arrangements be made to ensure that all dug-outs were provided with blankets for protection against gas. " Vermorel

C

sprayers must always be kept in working order and ready for use."

A Report from the General Staff 1st Corps was appended to the instructions of the Brigade Commander, with the usual cryptic remarks, so common in the Army on this class of document— " For your information and necessary action, please." The document mentioned said that a deserter had been captured on the night of the 23rd inst. on the corps front, and that the prisoner had made the following statement :—

" While there are no gas cylinders in the German front line " between the Hulluch-Vermelles road and the ' Quarries,' there " are gas cylinders on the front occupied by the 4th Bavarian " Division, that is to say, approximately between Puits 14 bis " and Hulluch." The deserter had also heard rumours, from overhearing officers conversing, about a proposed raid on the above front, to be made in considerable force, with the assistance of gas at a time when the wind would be favourable. The object of this raid, he gathered, was to secure identifications, and also to ascertain particulars regarding our mining system, and if possible to capture and destroy same. This information, the prisoner stated, was based mostly on hearsay, and he could not vouch for its reliability.

The C.O. circulated these documents for the perusal of company commanders on the evening of the 26th, but no immediate apprehension was felt regarding an impending attack.

Such were the incidents prior to the enemy gas attacks and minor operations of April 27th and 29th, 1916.

On the morning of the 27th April, shortly after 4-30 o'clock, the enemy opened up intense rifle and machine-gun fire opposite the centre of the divisional front, viz.—the 8th R.I.F., the 8th R.D.F. and ourselves.

A slight easterly breeze was blowing from the direction of the enemy, visibility was good, and altogether it was an excellent opportunity for the enemy to release gas and carry out a raid under cover of it.

About 4-45 a.m. our front, support and reserve lines were subjected to an intense hostile bombardment, and almost simultaneously the enemy released dense volumes of smoke and gas over the whole divisional front. With a favouring wind the gas cloud drifted across " No Man's Land " and over our trenches, and so exceedingly concentrated was it, that objects two or three yards away were rendered quite invisible.

For a time the cloud seemed to hang between the front and support lines, then gradually drifted in a south-westerly direction towards Loos, finally moving west over Mazingarbe towards Noeux-les-Mines. " A " Company, who were holding the reserve line, had a few minutes' warning of the approach of the gas cloud. Lieutenant H. W. Ruddock relates an amusing incident which occurred in relation to his platoon. Private Cassidy, who was changing his socks and was in his bare feet at the time, was ordered to put on his gas helmet. He did so, but put it on back to front. Rushing madly round the trench he kept clutching blindly at his helmet, and was heard to remark : " I wish I could find the b——— windows."

At 5-15 a.m. the bombardment was extended to the communications and the reserve and village lines. A large amount of lachrymatory shells were directed on Philosophe and batteries in the vicinity. Our guns by now were firing along the whole corps front.

At 5-40 a.m. the barrage fire increased in intensity, and under cover of this, and a second gas cloud, the enemy left their trenches in small parties along the front and succeeded in effecting a lodgment in various parts of the sector.

Opposite our immediate front the Germans left their trenches by a sap almost directly opposite " The Kink." Many became casualties in getting across " No Man's Land," but a party, under cover of the smoke, managed to get into our line at the junction of " B " and " C " Companies. Several of our men were killed and wounded in the hand-to-hand encounter which ensued, and a few, taken unawares, were made prisoners. Some of the men captured were killed in " No Man's Land " by our barrage. Captain R. N. Murray was undoubtedly taken at this point ; although he was not seen going across " No Man's Land " by an eye-witness, yet it was nevertheless, unfortunately, true, as a subsequent account showed that he had died in a German field hospital the following day from gas poisoning. On the right a party of the enemy got in somewhere in the region of Posen Alley. C.S.M. Pegram (" D " Company) and two men were captured by this party. The gas was so thick over this part of the trench that it was impossible to fix a definite point where the enemy effected an entrance. Owing to the prevalence of gas in the line it took some little time to organise an effective counter-attack. Captain V. H. Parr (" A " Company) who was in the reserve trench, realised that the situation in the front system was temporarily obscure, and on his own initiative sent up two platoons to reinforce " D " Company on the right. As it happened, these men were not required to expel the enemy, but were essential to the reorganising and strengthening of " D " Company, who had suffered very heavily from gas.

Major Ross White, who had been sent up by the C.O. from Battalion Headquarters at the commencement of the bombardment with a few men carrying ammunition and Vermorel solution, helped to clear up the situation on the right and to regain touch with the flank battalion which, owing to casualties, had been interrupted during the raid.

In the space of twenty minutes the raiders had been expelled and forced to retire back to their own line, subjected as they went to our rifle fire and shrapnel from the field guns.

The experiences of Captain R. G. Kerr (" B " Company), as recounted by himself, are worthy of record to give a clear and as accurate a description as possible of what happened on his left (junction of " C " and " B " Companies' front). He stated :—

" On the 27th, about half-an-hour after the second gas attack, I went down to the left of my company front where the raiders had got in.   I saw two of my men lying out in the wire, one was dead (Private Daye), the other I ordered to come in, which he did.   I asked him for an explanation as to why he had been there, and he (Private Bass) made the following statement :—He said he had been firing from a bay on the left of the company, and five or six unarmed men, presumably belonging to ' C ' Company, passed down the trench towards the right.   He did not recognise the men, and was amazed that they were unarmed.   Immediately behind them came a German officer and three men, who pointed their rifles at him and his comrade, ordering him to surrender, which he naturally had to do, taken unawares as he was from the flank.   At first the officer ordered him to fall in with the others, but another of them told him to get over the parapet and make for the German lines.   He did so, but his escort was killed almost immediately, and he remained in the wire until ordered to return by me."

The account of 9914 C.Q.M.S. Morrison (" C " Company), is interesting, and corroborates the above statement.   He says :
" I was with C.S.M. Coombes about fifteen minutes after the second
" gas attack, standing on a fire-step about twenty yards from the
" listening post to the right of Vendin Alley. Captain R. N. Murray
" was coming down the firing line from the left. I drew his atten-
" tion to the enemy retiring from our trenches on the right.   He
" left me and went to the right towards ' B ' Company.   That was
" the last I saw of him.   The enemy were in the trench at that
" time, because Mr. Milligan had come along and said they were.
" C.S.M. Coombes and myself carried on firing at the enemy as
" they withdrew across ' No Man's Land.'   I should think the
" raiders entered the trench just on the left of ' B ' Company's
" headquarters.   I saw the place afterwards they had used to
" get in."

At 6-10 a.m. the enemy blew a small mine between Munster and Tralee craters, but no action appeared to follow this blow. The enemy were now back in their own lines.

The divisional artillery, supplemented by the flank divisions, were now firing as fast as they could. The air shrieked with projectiles of every description. The " heavies " were firing shells of the railway-train variety, and made a continuous wail across the sky.

Communications by telephone were interrupted almost immediately after the commencement of the bombardment, and it was only with great difficulty, owing to the damaged state of the trenches, that runners could get their messages through. The runners and linemen undoubtedly did excellent service under most trying conditions.

Between 7-30 and 8 a.m. the enemy released more gas at various points along his front. Under cover of this cloud a second advance was attempted, but was not pushed with any vigour, and quickly died away. The wind had played him false, and the gas showed a tendency to drift back over themselves. Whether it was from the effect of his own gas or to avoid our artillery barrage is a matter of discussion, but the Germans climbed out of their front line and ran back over the top towards their support trench.

Lieutenant H. B. O. Mitchell and the Lewis gun teams under his command inflicted severe losses on the enemy during this action. He was afterwards awarded the Military Cross for his coolness and fine example of bravery.

By 8 a.m. the shelling had decreased considerably, and towards 11-30 a.m. the sector was silent. The stinking fumes of chlorine still hung throughout the trenches. Our line was now battered and smashed out of all recognition. Duckboards smashed up, communications destroyed and blocked up with shell craters, material of every description, hurled sky-high during the bombardment, now lay scattered about the area like so much flotsam and jetsam.

Everywhere wounded and gassed men staggering, walking, or limping on each other's shoulders, towards the aid post. Here and there a fire bay full of dead would tell its own tale. All day a ceaseless stream of wounded and gassed were brought down Vendin Alley to the regimental aid post in Curzon Street. Nothing could exceed the care and devotion shown by the medical officer (Captain G. O. F. Alley, R.A.M.C.) in attending to those coming in, directing bearers, allotting places and evacuating the wounded to the casualty clearing stations. Corporal Chasty, Privates Smyth, Mooney, Potter, McCluskey and others on the medical staff went up to the line time after time bringing down the wounded and badly gassed.

Out of a total of 24 officers and 603 other ranks who came into the line with the battalion, no less than 10 officers and 253 other ranks were casualties.   A detail of the casualties is given below :—

COMPANY	KILLED	WOUNDED	MISSING	GASSED	TOTALS
" A "	3	5	–	20	28
" B "	28	10	2	50	90
" C "	18	13	3	39	73
" D "	17	24	3	28	72
	66	52	8	137	263

So many and varied were the cases of devotion to duty and individual acts of gallantry by all ranks, it would be quite impossible to enumerate them all.   Captain J. Ritty (" B " Company) was awarded the Military Cross, as was Lieutenant H. B. O. Mitchell (" C " Company).   C.S.M. Coombes (" C " Company) and Private Hugh Robinson (" C " Company) and Private P. Brown (" B " Company) all received recognition for their bravery.

The night of the 27th passed quietly, and our patrols did much useful work in " No Man's Land."   Several men who at first had been reported missing were found.   Some who had been wounded and gassed were brought safely back to our lines.   Lieutenant A. L'E. Brownlow (" A " Company) and Lieutenant M. J. Daly did good work in collecting identifications from the dead Germans lying out there.   The work of clearing the ground was also being carried out by the enemy, so great care had to be exercised to avoid detection.

On the morning of the 28th, the battalion was relieved by the 8th Battalion Royal Inniskilling Fusiliers, and moved into Brigade support in 10th Avenue.   " B " Company (Captain R. G. Kerr) took over the garrison of a forward reserve position, the other companies remained in 10th Avenue.

Our troubles were not over yet, for, at dawn on the 29th April, the enemy launched another attack, though at the time it was impossible from 10th Avenue to locate it, as the whole area was resounding with the S.O.S. gas alarm from Klaxton and Strombos horns.   The enemy artillery was active, but not concentrated on us.   Promiscuous whizz-bangs and 5.9's were coming in our direction.   In front the barrage sounded heavy.   The following report by the C.O. addressed to Headquarters, 49th Infantry

Brigade, and dated the 29/4/16, gives a chronological detail of events during the attack on that date :—

" HEADQUARTERS.   R 1117.

" 49TH INFANTRY BRIGADE.

" REPORT ON ATTACK, 29/4/16.

" As it appeared to this battalion.   At 3-55 a.m. heavy gun
" fire was directed by Germans on the ' Quarry Sector.'
" At 4 a.m. S.O.S. signal gas was received from Brigade Head-
" quarters by telephone, though no gas was noticeable in 10th
" Avenue until 4-10 a.m.
" At 4-15 a.m. enemy's gun fire sensibly decreased.
" At 4-26 a.m. Pike (code name of 7th Royal Irish Fusiliers)
" reported apparent gas attack, and all communications cut by
" shell fire.
" At 4-28 a.m. Perch (8th Royal Inniskilling Fusiliers) asked for
" a company to support them.
" At 4-55 a.m. ' B ' Company (Captain R. G. Kerr) reported
" they had been heavily gassed.
" At 5 a.m. enemy's gun fire practically ceased.
" At 5-12 a.m. 10th Avenue was free from gas.
" Vague reports continued to be received for the rest of the
" morning prophesying another attack, or actually declaring it had
" commenced.
" Reports received from battalions in support of brigades on
" either flank discredited these reports.
" My own *two companies also reassured me that nothing
" serious was on—in fact, apart from gas, it would appear no
" Germans left their trenches on our front.
" The gas attack seemed to be merely a form of offensive,
" defensive on the enemy's part to tie us and our supports to
" this area, whilst he raided elsewhere.
" At 7-28 a.m. a report was received *re* the disablement of two
" Lewis guns and their teams in ' the kink,' and I reported this to
" you at 7-45 a.m.
" At 11-15 a.m. a German aeroplane fell about 800 yards to the
" left rear of Battalion Headquarters.

" (Signed) H. N. YOUNG, *Lieut.-Colonel.*

" Dated 29/4/16."

---

* This would appear to refer to " A " and " B " Companies.

When the C.O. of the 8th Inniskillings asked for support, the Colonel ordered Major Reid and " C " Company to go to his assistance.   The company was not eventually required, as the enemy's artillery had ceased, and the attack had been repulsed. " B " Company suffered very heavily during the bombardment and the gas attack on this day.   Their casualties are included in the aforementioned table.

The battalion was relieved on the same night by the 7th Camerons, and moved into Philosophe West.   The 8th R.I.F., who had come out of the line the night before, provided us with a hot meal and, thanks to their hospitality, billets also, and sleep was appreciated by us all.

The following day was spent by the orderly room in estimating and checking casualty returns, collecting and collating reports from the companies, and consolidating various returns and indents for lost and damaged material.   The men spent their day washing and shaving, and generally cleaning up arms and equipment. Buttons had been rendered black by the action of the gas, and rifles were to a large extent polluted by it.   In the evening the following orders were issued by the C.O. :—

" SPECIAL ORDERS."

By Lieutenant-Colonel H. N. Young, Commanding 7th (S.) Battalion Royal Inniskilling Fusiliers.

30/4/16.

The following telegram was sent to all companies on the 28th inst., at 9-45 a.m., with reference to the fighting on the morning of the 27th April :—

" The Army Commander, General Sir Charles Monro, has " telephoned to congratulate the 49th Infantry Brigade on their " gallant conduct on the morning of the 27th inst.

" The Divisional Commander, Major-General Hickie, also tele- " phones to say how proud he is of their behaviour.

" The above messages apply chiefly to the two battalions of " the brigade in the firing line.   Further, the brunt of the " attack would appear to have fallen on the 7th Royal Inniskilling " Fusiliers."

The C.O. received the following personal letter from Major-General W. B. Hickie, C.B., Commanding the 16th (Irish) Division, on the 28th inst. :—

" I am directed by Sir Charles Monro, Commanding the 1st Army, to convey to you and to the Officers, N.C.O's. and men of the battalion under your command, his appreciation of the conduct of the battalion on the occasion of the German attack on April

27th. To these congratulations I wish also to add my own thanks.

"The C.O. desires on his own behalf to express to all ranks his high appreciation of their conduct and bearing on the 27th and 29th instant, when they displayed a high standard of courage and endurance, and showed themselves worthy upholders of the traditions of the Royal Inniskilling Fusiliers.

"(Signed) A. C. Taggart, Captain and Adjutant,
"7th (S.) Battalion Royal Inniskilling Fusiliers."

On the afternoon of the 1st May, the officers and other ranks who had been killed in the recent operations, and others who had succumbed to gas poisoning, were laid to rest in the battalion cemetery at Philosophe East. The C.O., adjutant and many of the battalion attended the funeral service, which was conducted by Father Doyle.

On the 3rd inst., Brigadier-General R. Leveson-Gower commanding the 49th Infantry Brigade, came over to billets and inspected the battalion on parade. Only 14 officers and 300 men were on parade. The General, having been received with the "general salute," addressed a few words to the battalion :

"Officers, W.O's., N.C.O's. and men of the 7th Royal Innis-
"killing Fusiliers, I admire your bravery and the courage you have
"shown since you have taken your place in the line, and especially
"on the 27th and 29th of April.

"When defending a position under a storm of shrapnel, high
"explosive, etc. and at the same time being subjected to three gas
"attacks, as you were on the 27th inst., it is easy to get excited
"and cause a panic. You, however, stood firm, counter-attacked,
"and absolutely defeated the enemy's attack. You have seen
"the worst of it, and have shown by your steadiness, coolness,
"and courage that you were good soldiers.

"Our time will come when we shall advance, and you will then
"have a chance, no doubt, of inflicting punishment on the enemy.

"By the fighting you have gone through, you have found out
"one thing, namely, that the officers you have are good men,
"whom you can trust, and with them you will get along all right,
"and at the same time you, officers, have found your men to be
"true and resolute.

"The other battalions of the brigade feel confident when they
"have you beside them.

"You have proved yourselves good men of your country.
"Ireland can be proud of you, and in the future, when asked what
"battalion did you belong to, you can answer with pride that you

" were in the 7th Battalion Royal Inniskilling Fusiliers, *a real*
" *fighting battalion,* and you need say nothing further. I thank
" you very much, knowing I can rely on you wherever you go."

Three of the heartiest cheers were then given for the General,
and the parade dismissed.

  *   *   *   *   *   *   *   *

On the evening of the 4th-5th May we relieved the 8th K.O.S.B.
in Tenth Avenue, and the companies were disposed as follows :—

   " A " Company (Captain V. H. Parr)—Posen Alley to Lone
    Tree Redoubt.
   " B " Company (Captain R. G. Kerr)—Lone Tree Redoubt.
   " C " Company (Major Reid)—From Lone Tree Redoubt
    to Hay Alley.
   " D " Company (Captain Sutton)—From Hay Alley to
    Hulluch Road.

The relief was carried out and completed before dusk, which
necessitated companies moving up independently, via Northern Up.
This entailed very slow progress and invariably meant getting
into the communication trench as far back as Philosophe. At
night the battalion could move across country or along the
Lens Road to within 1,000 yards of the front line.

Two days completed the tour in support, during which time
the situation was normal. Relief came on the night of the 6th-7th.
The 7th Royal Irish Rifles relieved, and the battalion moved back
to Noeux-les-Mines for eight days' rest.

In divisional reserve the battalion had better billets and more
facilities for general cleaning-up and reorganising. The word
" rest," however, hardly conveys a true picture of the scene. In
some respects these periods of " rest " were more strenuous than
a tour in the front system. Fatigue parties were required every
night to go up the line, and the only units available were the
battalions of the Reserve brigade in Mazingarbe and Noeux respectively. Night after night companies marched up to the Loos
Salient for different employments. Some would be detailed as
carrying parties or ration bearers to the forward system, others
for the never-ending trench construction and repair duties under
the supervision of the R.E. The most irksome part of these
fatigues was the marching to and from the line, for Noeux was a
good five miles from the trench zone, and most of the way was
pavé road, which at this time of the year was particularly
tiring on the men.

Needless to say, training was practically negligible during these
periods of reserve, except for Lewis gunners, signallers and others
specially employed. Working parties seldom returned to billets
before dawn, which meant that most of the day was given up to

rest and cleaning of equipment. These days of all-work and very little time for sport and recreation made us almost mechanical in our duties and impervious to our surroundings. The arrival of the letters from home, the perusal of the English papers, and the prospect of leave—sometime—were the only thoughts to distract our minds from the dull monotony and unutterable boredom of trench warfare. Day in and day out the same everlasting routine. Had it not been for the tremendous personal energy and activity of the C.O., apathy and lethargy, with their concomitant evils, might have crept in. No work, no trouble could ever conquer our C.O. All day long he would keep a vigilant eye on everyone's movements. In the orderly room he was for ever writing reports, thinking out schemes for annoying the enemy, and interviewing his Officers and N.C.O's. Nothing escaped him, and no crime went unpunished ; the officers and staff of Battalion Headquarters knew this to their cost. An absurdly amusing incident happened one day at the " orderly room " when the C.O. sentenced the officers' mess cook to fourteen days' field imp-isonment No. 1. The mess president was naturally full of apprehension as to how and where he would get the meals cooked. All day he rushed from one company commander to another in search of a cook. The C.O. very soon solved the difficulty for him. The convicted cook was brought up to the mess daily under an escort of two policemen, cooked the meals for the day, and was then led back to the guard room at night.

The 9th of May will ever be memorable to the battalion and the inhabitants of Noeux for the great " dummy raid " carried out by us on the training ground in the vicinity. No amount of ammunition, rockets, Verey lights or bombs were spared to make the enterprise look as realistic as possible. To a mere spectator it must have looked like a gigantic firework display ; to the participants it was both amusing and instructive. The raiding party was commanded by Major Reid, and the raided consisted of detachments of " C " and " D " Companies, to represent the enemy.

The operations commenced about 10 p.m. by a pre-arranged signal from the " British Lines " given by the C.O. On receiving this signal, the " enemy " fired occasional flares, together with a few rounds of " blank," to represent the normal action in trench warfare.

On the firing of a green Verey light, the " enemy," who had squads of bombers previously told off for their duties, commenced to throw live bombs as a representation of the " British " barrage. Each barrage party consisted of an N.C.O. and one bomber, who were given twenty-four " Mills " to perform the task.

On the cessation of the " barrage," the " British," who had been waiting in " No Man's Land," advanced to the attack.

The scheme was carried out quite successfully, though at the time many of the civilians must have thought the Boche had broken through. R.S.M. Dolan took as much delight in firing off the " S.O.S." rockets as anyone who took part in the proceeding. Luckily the casualties were light, and after the " cease fire " sounded, the C.O. gave a short discourse on the lessons learnt, and we marched back to billets and bed.

On the night of the 11th, at 6-50 o'clock, the battalion got orders to " stand to " and be ready to move up the line at an hour's notice. This order was not cancelled until the the following morning, but in the meantime we were not called on during the night. Ordinary training was proceeded with until the 17th, when we moved up to the Loos Sector. On the night of the 17th-18th we took over the line, with the companies disposed as follows :—

> " D " Company (Captain Sutton)—North Street to Gordon Alley.
> " A " Company (Captain Parr)—Gordon Alley to Scots Alley.
> " C " Company (Major Reid)—Scots Alley to English Alley.

Each company in the firing line found its own supports.

" B " Company (Captain Kerr) was in reserve in the cellars north of Scots Alley.

Battalion Headquarters was situated in a dilapidated farm-house to the west of the village of Loos, about twenty yards east of English Alley.

Though it was now nearly two months since we had actually held the Loos Sector proper, the sector was not unfamiliar to us. Perhaps the village looked a little more desolated and ruined, if that were possible. It had been a typical mining village of Northern France, and the population of the village must have consisted for the most part of mine workers. The great spider-webbed iron tower of the mine was still standing, though the enemy had hurled every projectile imaginable against it to destroy it. So far he had not succeeded, but by the end of May he brought it to the ground. Needless to relate, the village was a mass of skeleton cottages and *debris* of masonry and bricks. Though the accommodation in the cellars was still ample to afford cover for troops, the village was very little used in this respect, most wisely no doubt, as the enemy could have made it very unpleasant had he wished. With the exception of our Battalion Headquarters, and that of the Right Battalion in the post office, there were very few troops billeted in the village. The divisional pioneers garrisoned the defences on the outskirts of the town, but were mostly confined to the north-west corner, where they were comparatively unmolested.

It was extraordinary, taking into consideration the numbers of men who went through the village daily carrying rations and material, how few casualties we sustained from shell or rifle fire. At night the Germans enfiladed the streets with spasmodic bursts of indirect machine-gun fire and stray rifle shots at frequent intervals, obviously in the hope of inflicting casualties. The damage done by this action was inappreciable, though it made one quicken one's steps passing the danger spots. After dusk each evening the battalion transport, accompanied by Lieutenant H. F. Reid (Transport Officer) and Lieutenant W. Reid (Quartermaster), would bring up the daily supplies of rations, ammunition and other requisites, as far as Crucifix Dump. Here they were met by the battalion parties, distributed, and carried up to the respective companies.

On the 19th, Captain A. L'E. Brownlow was severely wounded, and evacuated. Though he never returned to the battalion we were pleased to hear that he made a complete recovery.

On the 21st-22nd, the battalion was relieved by the 8th Inniskillings, and moved into support. The companies were then disposed as follows, and became for tactical purposes under the command of the O.C. front system :—

"B" Company (Captain Kerr)—In the cellars about G.35. d.6.5.

"C" Company (Major Reid)—In the cellars north of Scots Alley.

"D" Company (Captain Sutton)—In the cellars north of the enclosure.

"A" Company (Captain Parr) and Battalion Headquarters —In the village line (Tenth Avenue).

During our four days in support, Captain C. H. Stainforth rejoined the battalion (having been gassed on the 27th April) and resumed command of "D" Company.

On the 25th-26th, the battalion moved up to the front system again, taking over from the 8th Battalion with the same dispositions as hitherto, with the exception that "D" Company was in reserve. The following day, owing to the enormously decreased strength of the companies from previous casualties, it was decided by the Divisional Commander to lend us the 16th Divisional Cyclist Company. They were accordingly put in the cellars north of Scots Alley in local reserve.

A special company for raiding purposes, comprised of one officer and a proportion of other ranks from each company to the total of fifty, was withdrawn from the line for training. Major Reid took command of this party, and they moved to billets in Mazingarbe on the 27th May.

On the night of the relief the enemy blew a " camouflet " in our mining galleries, near Seaforth Crater, on " C " Company's front.   C.S.M. Kernan and Corporal J. Rainey did excellent work in going down the mine shaft and rescuing men who had been gassed by the explosion.   The C.O. recommended this W.O. and N.C.O. very strongly for their brave and determined action, and they received the award of the Military Medal.

The general situation during this tour was " normal " for such a sector as Loos, though the continuous exchange of rifle grenades and trench mortars, coupled with the ever-present anxiety of the enemy blowing a mine under our front line, made life rather unpleasant at times. The responsibility and tension of the company commander was very great on account of these mines.   He had ever to be on the look out for any unusual activity on his own front.   Captain Stainforth while patrolling one of his front line posts one evening was convinced that mining operations were in progress under his very parapet.   He hastily summoned his flank company commanders to the spot to consult with them and take their advice as to clearing that particular portion of trench so as to preserve his company from being decimated.   With the help of the other two he soon discovered the " mine ; " a rat had been boring a home for its family in the sand-bags.

But Battalion Headquarters never stopped to think of mines under them.   Some new work was always going on.   Besides the usual amount of trench states, situation reports, telegraph messages and chits on all subjects from " men's feet " to their rations, the C.O. decided on improving his headquarters.   He was determined he should have a stronghold that would resist any shell the enemy could make or had made.   Signallers, clerks, orderlies, batmen, all had their share in this new dug-out.   At first the C.O. was content to make a " burster " on the cellar, but when that was finished, a new battle headquarters was to be made, so that it would accommodate the signal *personnel* as well.   The work was eventually completed to the satisfaction of everybody concerned, and to crown the paradise Sergeant McNulty, the pioneer sergeant, painted a very ostentatious-looking board and erected it over the door, with the title of " Fort Inniskilling."   It became well known later throughout the sector.   Perhaps it still remains—who knows ?

The battalion was relieved by the 5th Royal Berks Regiment on the night 29th-30th May.

*   *   *   *   *   *   *   *

Major A. D. Reid, whilst commanding " C " Company in the Loos Salient, wrote a brief account of the company commander's " point of view."   The narrative which is published below is a typical episode of an everyday occurrence in the trenches :—

" The company commander sat in his dug-out.   His last

subaltern had just been sent on a course for darning socks. A guttering candle gave the only light that relieved the gloom, and large drops of water fell with a relentless splash here and there and round about it. Indeed, it was a wonder it did not get hit. At one end of the dug-out could be heard the murmurs of servants talking in a low tone over a charcoal brazier, from which was escaping the sizzle and smell of bacon frying ; it was near breakfast hour. At the other end the buzz of the telephone vented its mosquito-like hum in a leisurely way. But suddenly, in a flash, the buzz-buzz became crisp and decided. A message was coming through—buzz—buzz, buzz, buzz.

" ' What the devil is it now,' thought the company commander.

" In a few minutes a figure loomed up. ' Sir, the Adjutant wants to speak to an officer of the company on the 'phone.'

" ' All right, I'm coming.'

" From outside. A crash ! ! Bang ! ! The dug-out shook with the concussion. ' I ought to go up and see what's going on.'

" ' The Adjutant is waiting, sir.'

" Boom ! Bang ! ! Crash ! ! ! The dug-out shook outrageously.

" ' I must go up. The Adjutant can wait.'

" Up above, the parapet was flying about in little pieces. The trench was being shelled by heavies, strafed by rifle-grenades, and peppered with pip-squeaks. The company commander sped round and encouraged the men to spread out and take cover. For their part they were more or less indifferent. Here one was frying bacon on a biscuit tin converted into a brazier ; there another boiling tea in a mess tin. Bang ! Over goes the tea. Patiently and with a jest he proceeds to build up his kitchenette anew. Bang ! Another bit of parapet leaps out and deposits Private M'Mifty on his back on the floor of the trench.

" ' Begorrah, sir,' says he, ' they've put me off my seat.'

" For twenty minutes the company commander darts up and down the trench. Then the strafing ceases.

" ' Thank God, no casualties,' he says, as he wipes the sweat off his brow and returns to the dug-out.

" The Adjutant is again calling up with obvious irritation.

" ' The C.O. wishes to know why there is no officer at the 'phone.'

" ' Yes.'

" ' Tell him we were being strafed.'

" ' Yes, had to go on deck.'

" ' Yes, no other officer available.'

" ' Yes. By the way, what is it you want ? '

" ' C. O. wishes you to detail an officer for a course of instruction in ' the use of trench gloves.'

" Fizz ! A larger drop than usual has registered a direct hit on the candle, and all is darkness and stifled words in the dug-out."

CHAPTER IV.

To be relieved by a battalion of the " Berks " was unusual.
The reason for this was that the 8th Royal Inniskilling Fusiliers,
who were generally our " opposite number " for relief, had gone
away for a fortnight to the seaside to recuperate after the gas
attack of the 29th of April.

It was a long and protracted relief, which was not complete
until 2 o'clock the following morning. Harassing fire directed
on English Alley and the cellars of Pip Street was to a large
extent the cause of delay, to add to which the communications
were interrupted owing to the enemy activity. The C.O. lost
interest and patience with the " signal service " shortly after
midnight, and his usual commentaries regarding the telephone
system were peculiarly caustic on this occasion. The signal
officer remained at headquarters to report to Brigade Headquarters the completion of relief, and the C.O. (Captain Taggart),
with the faithful orderlies, McHale and Rigby, left for Philosophe
East. Two companies, on being relieved (" A " and " D ") were
detailed to remain in close support near Loos, the remainder,
with Battalion Headquarters, marched to billets in Philosophe
East and brigade reserve.

Two days were spent in Philosophe, uneventful and monotonous.
During the day, save for the usual rifle and gas respirator

inspections, the men were given the privilege of being allowed a little respite. At night came the everlasting carrying-party fatigues and working parties for the line. Our chief duty was to supply sufficient men to push the trucks along the Decauville Railway from Victoria Station to Posen Dump, where the various battalion ration parties collected their supplies after dusk.

On the morning of the 2nd June, the battalion marched to billets in Noeux-les-Mines to remain for eight days in divisional reserve. "A" and "D" Companies, who were still in occupation of the village lines and Lens Road Redoubt, were relieved by the 9th Royal Dublin Fusiliers, and rejoined the battalion in Noeux later in the evening.

An interesting event in the history of the battalion was marked by the recognition of the Graves Registration Committee of the battalion cemetery at Philosophe East. Unfortunately, the cemetery had grown considerably during the last few months, and now consisted of nearly sixty graves in all. It was gratifying to the C.O., who had himself shown such personal interest in the upkeep of the battalion burial ground, to see that the men appreciated the idea so much. Almost every day when we were in brigade reserve the men would spend their leisure moments tending the graves of their comrades and their friends.

During our eight days in rest, the Corps Commander, Lieutenant-General C. T. McM. Cavanagh, bestowed the ribbons of their respective decorations on the following *personnel* who had served with distinction in the operations of the 27th and 29th of April :— Second-Lieutenant H. B. O. Mitchell received the Military Cross ; Privates Brown and Robinson were presented with the Military Medal. Captain J. Ritty and 29114 A/C.S.M. G. Coombes, having been evacuated to England suffering from gas poisoning, were unable to be present.

On the 6th inst. the Army Commander, Sir Charles Monro, had expressed his intention of inspecting the battalion, but at the last minute, owing to unforeseen circumstances, the parade was cancelled. The Colonel, in his absence, distributed the following Officers, W.O.'s, N.C.O.'s and men with the " Parchment of the Irish Division," bestowed on them by the Divisional Commander in appreciation of their services rendered, and magnificent behaviour during the enemy gas attack at Hulluch :—

> Major R. Ross White (Second in Command).
> Captain A. C. Taggart (Adjutant).
> Major A. D. Reid (" C " Company).
> Lieutenant G. O. F. Alley, R.A.M.C. (M.O.)
> Lieutenant G. A. C. Walker (Signal Officer).
> Lieutenant E. N. Flook.

Lieutenant R. T. Sutton.
Lieutenant C. Lefevre.
Second-Lieutenant H. B. O. Mitchell, M.C. (Lewis gun
    Officer.)
Captain J. Ritty, M.C.
Second-Lieutenant A. E. C. Trimble.
29114 A/C.S.M. G. Coombes.
13133 A/R.S.M. R. Dolan.
13445 A/Sergeant G. Dunne.
16520 A/Corporal J. J. M'Guinness.
22780 Lance-Corporal C. Cochrane.
24180 Private J. Maguire.
26288 Private P. Brown.
23618 Private F. Smyth.
23325 Private H. Robinson, M.M.
22505 Private P. Brown, M.M.

After the distribution the Commanding Officer made a short
speech, in the course of which he expressed the wish that all
ranks would for ever try to improve themselves as soldiers and
men. " Do not imagine for a moment," he said, " that you
cannot be better than you are. Nothing is, or can be, too good
for a Royal Inniskilling Fusilier."

On the night of the 10th-11th the battalion moved up the
line, and took over the left sub-sector of " Puits 14 bis "—Vendin
Alley (North) to Boyau 60, immediately north of the Chalk Pit.
Three companies were detailed to the front line in the following
order :—

" D " Company (Captain Sutton), left.
" B " Company (Captain R. G. Kerr), centre.
" C " Company (Major Reid), right.
" A " Company (Captain V. H. Parr) occupied the reserve
    trench.

Battalion Headquarters in Curzon Street.

This tour was particularly noticeable for the enormously
increased use of " Minnies " by the enemy, not only by day,
but to a considerable extent after dark. Although the casualties
inflicted by these heavy trench mortars were not in any way
proportional to the amount of enemy ammunition expended,
yet the damage to our trenches and the deafening detonations
were factors in themselves, which had a bad effect on the *morale*
of the garrison. To attempt to counteract this activity by
means of retaliation from our medium trench mortars was not
feasible, first, because the communications to the officers commanding those sections was extremely difficult to maintain,
and consequently unreliable ; secondly, the supply of ammunition
at this time was extremely limited, and no scheme on a small

The Irish Brigade

I HAVE READ WITH MUCH PLEASURE THE REPORTS OF YOUR REGIMENTAL COMMANDER AND BRIGADE COMMANDER REGARDING YOUR GALLANT CONDUCT AND DEVOTION TO DUTY IN THE FIELD ON _____ AND HAVE ORDERED YOUR NAME AND DEED TO BE ENTERED IN THE RECORD OF THE IRISH DIVISION.

Major-General,
Commanding 16th Irish Division.

PARCHMENT CERTIFICATE OF THE
16TH (IRISH) DIVISION.

scale could have had any appreciable effect. The artillery
did what they could (by using code words for the different mortars
in action) to identify and locate their positions and harass the
personnel when in action. This scheme was partially successful,
but did little or no damage to the enemy mortars. The Boche,
needless to say, had his " Minnenwerfers " well concealed in
deep and well-fortified concreted emplacements, and practically
immune from our field artillery fire.

The G.O.C. of the Brigade, who had direct control of the L.T.M.
batteries, ordered a certain percentage of Stoke's ammunition
to be fired daily in " retaliation." This was very often effective,
but was not to be relied on to any extent, as the enemy could
silence our Stokes whenever he wished, owing to the fact that
they were so unprotected in their hastily-constructed trench
emplacements.

A great drawback to the " Stoke's retaliation method " was
the fact that it drew fire on some particular portion of the
front very often, thereby causing unnecessary casualties. An
amusing example of the anxiety of the company commander
for his men and his aversion to the activity of the over-keen
trench mortar officer is afforded by the personal encounter of
Lieutenant M. J. Daly and the Commander of " C " Company
(Lieutenant C. Lefevre).

It was a particularly quiet day on our front, and Lieutenant
Daly was ordered to fire two hundred rounds on a certain target,
within range of the top of Posen Alley. With trepidation, the
L.T.M. Commander explained his mission to the O. C. " C "
Company. At first the company commander received him as
a friend, but ascertaining the purport of his plan, he entreated
him not to fire, offering him at the same time all the hospitality
he could afford, even to the extent of lending him a party to
" bury the ammunition " if it came to a point of getting rid of it.
Lieutenant Daly was firm and resolute in his purpose, but tact-
fully withdrew on being threatened to be put under arrest
should a man of " C " Company be hit by enemy retaliation.
The shoot was successful, and did not draw unusual retaliation
on the offended company commander.

On the night of the 15th-16th the battalion was relieved by
the 8th Inniskillings, after we had attempted a minor enterprise
in the vicinity of Posen Crater. The operation was carried out,
unfortunately, without sufficient preparation, and through
unforeseen circumstances was unsuccessful. On the afternoon
of the 15th inst. the C.O. received orders to carry out a
raid on the enemy's system, for the purpose of obtaining an
identification from the troops opposite, and if possible to capture
some prisoners. The portion of the front selected by the C.O.

for the scheme was immediately south of Posen Crater to a sap some hundred yards further south. Major Reid was given command of the party, and a bangalore torpedo section was provided to blow a gap in the enemy's wire. It might be well to point out, without unduly criticising the general outline of the scheme, that nobody in the battalion—not even the C.O.—had ever seen or heard of a bangalore torpedo, and consequently did not know its powers and limitations.

Battalion Headquarters was naturally unusually active for the remainder of the afternoon ; details connected with the relief had to be settled, and at the same time special operation orders had to be issued concerning the raid. The C.O. and the adjutant worked indefatigably throughout the afternoon, whilst Major A. D. Reid got busy in selecting his officers and men for the enterprise. Major Rudkin (Brigade Major) visited the C.O. at about 7 o'clock and later accompanied the C.O. to the front line to assist and witness the operations. Major Rudkin's quick decision and clear judgment at all times won him the respect of all the officers in the battalion.

The party, when finally selected for the scheme, consisted of Second-Lieutenant H. B. O. Mitchell, M.C., Second-Lieutenant J. B. Watson (recently joined) and about forty Other Ranks. Arrangements were completed by 2-30 o'clock the following morning, and at 2-55 o'clock the commander of the raiding party ordered the bangalore torpedo to be fired. Second-Lieutenant H. B. O. Mitchell, M.C., who was on the left of the main body, noticed a party advancing towards him on his left flank. Twenty to twenty-five Germans were approaching through the long grass in " No Man's Land." Fearing lest the whole raiding party should be cut off, he gave the signal to retire, which was a red Verey light. The bangalore party and Second-Lieutenant Watson, on seeing the signal, quickly withdrew to our own line. The retirement gave the idea away to the enemy, and he immediately raked their path of retreat with machine-gun fire. Some minutes later, his field artillery was in action, and concentrated on our front line. Second-Lieutenant Watson was mortally wounded by shell fire, and though he was conveyed with all speed to the aid post, he died the following day at Bethune. He was interred in the battalion cemetery at Philosophe.

On completion of relief, the battalion moved into Brigade support in Tenth Avenue. The position taken up by the companies was from the junction of the village line with Tenth Avenue to Lone Trench. Battalion Headquarters was situated in the village line, midway between Chalk Pit Alley and Posen Alley— a most unattractive and evil-smelling spot, with very limited dug-out accommodation.

The four days spent in Brigade support were unusually arduous for the men. A carrying party, consisting of the whole battalion, with the C.O. and adjutant in charge, was employed in carrying up gas cylinders from Posen Dump to the front line. So careful were the staff that there would be no leakage of information regarding them, these cylinders were only referred to in orders or in conversation by their code name, " Loos Wallers." The work of distributing these " Loos Wallers " in the various sectors was a very trying and patience-wearing proceeding, for two reasons : first, they were so infernally heavy and cumbersome, and secondly, they were so vulnerable to splinters and bullets. The latter, of course, would mean death to the carriers if a cylinder happened to be pierced. Happily their transport was efficiently and satisfactorily carried out, assisted, like many things, by a degree of good luck.

The night of the 20th-21st saw us back again in the front line sector we had vacated only four days previously. A change was made, however, in our dispositions. The whole battalion held the front line with a company of the 8th Battalion attached for tactical purposes in reserve trench (Vendin Alley to Posen Alley).

To appreciate the reason for this strengthening of the garrison, the sudden appearance of gas cylinders in the front line, and the recent attempts to raid the enemy for identifications, one must bear in mind that the British were on the eve of their Great Push, which, though it was more or less common knowledge that it would be launched somewhere south, yet every effort was being made along the whole British front to make the enemy believe that it wasn't where he might imagine it was going to be, and at the same time stop the enemy moving troops by our constant aggressive activity. With these points in view, it did not come as a surprise that we were ordered to dig assembly trenches under cover of darkness on the night of the 21st. The line selected by the G.O.C. was about two hundred yards west of the support line, running parallel (north and south) across Broadway. The object of this to the enemy was obvious, or at any rate, it was meant to make-believe that we contemplated an attack on a large scale. Similar activity took place on our flank divisions. Harassing fire from our artillery increased perceptibly—in fact, no opportunity was missed to annoy and disturb the enemy as much as possible. The result of deceiving the enemy appeared satisfactory from later accounts. The offensive activity was brought to a climax in the most successful and efficient raid, carried out by the 7th Leinster Regiment, about a fortnight later in the vicinity of Loos.

Relief by the 8th Battalion came on the night of the 22nd-23rd, and the battalion moved once more into Tenth Avenue and Brigade support. Dispositions were similar to those held previously. The C.O. moved Battalion Headquarters further south to better accommodation and a more suitable location,

Normal trench warfare in Tenth Avenue was not unpleasant by any means, as it was quite a rare occurrence for the Hun to shell it, unless, of course, a raid or some local enterprise was taking place. The reason for this comparative immunity from shell fire was because there was no direct observation on it from the enemy's lines, though, no doubt, if he wanted to " shoot it up " he could have done so with the assistance of aircraft and observation balloons. True, the dug-out accommodation was sufficient in most cases for the garrison ; on the other hand, it was dirty and infested with rats. Tenth Avenue was, correctly speaking, the old German front line prior to the Battle of Loos (September, 1915), which had now been converted by the British as a support position. Fire-steps had been dug on the reverse side, traverses put in order, and a formidable belt of wire erected in front of it. The line itself had been so battered and knocked about by our artillery at the Battle of Loos, and the demolition being carried on by the severity of winter, it was doubtful if it would ever have withstood a counter-offensive if pushed home with any vigour. Small working parties were employed on deepening and fortifying the local redoubts daily, and did much during the summer months to put the line in a good state of defence.

On the 25th of June, the C.O. attended a conference at Battalion Headquarters in Curzon Street ; the result of which was an order by the Brigadier to carry out a raid (under cover of a gas cloud) on the evening of the 26th on the enemy's line opposite Boyeaux 67 and 68, better described, perhaps, as midway between Vendin Alley and " The Kink." It was decided that smoke bombs, " P " bombs and the discharge from the " Loos Wallers " should be used to cover the attack, provided the wind (which at the time was favourable) remained so.

Captain C. H. Stainforth was given command of the raiding party, and the following officers and W.O.'s were detailed with him :—Lieutenant H. B. O. Mitchell, M.C., Second-Lieutenant J. Cunningham, Second-Lieutenant C. A. Crowe and Second-Lieutenant Shaw ; C.S.M. McKeman and C.S.M. Knibbs. At 10 p.m. the raiding party set out for their assembly position in the support line (between Vendin Alley and Broadway) fully equipped with knobkerries, bombs, and, to complete their paraphernalia, their faces were blackened to avoid detection. The wind played false about an hour before zero, and the G.O.C. Brigade had to cancel the scheme.

On the morning of the 26th, the battalion was relieved by the 7th Royal Irish Rifles, and marched back to Mazingarbe by companies in daylight, via Northern Up and Philosophe. The huts at Mazingarbe were never appreciated for rest in the same way as those at Noeux-les-Mines. The village was small and very dirty, and with the exception of two or three small " estaminets," which kept watered beer in large quantities, there was nothing to see and very little to do when off duty. Fatigues were never-ending, not only by night, but often parties had to be detailed during the day to strengthen and improve the back defences of the so-called Army and G.H.Q. lines.

On the 3rd July the battalion moved up once more into the support of the Loos Sector. An unpleasant incident, which might have been attended with unfortunate results, occurred. As we were about to move off, the enemy started to shell the camp with " pip-squeaks," at what must have been almost his extreme range. One or two huts were knocked about, but otherwise no damage was done. The Boche was just ten minutes' too late.

The dispositions of the battalion in support during this trip were unusual, and are worthy of notice in considering the existing demands of the situation at the time :—

    " A " Company in the cellars of the Enclosure (Loos).

    " B " Company in the cellars of Pip Street (tactically under the command of the 8th Royal Inniskilling Fusiliers).

    " D " Company in the cellars of the Enclosure (tactically under the command of the 7th Royal Irish Fusiliers).

    " C " Company and Battalion Headquarters in Duke Street (from Railway Alley on the north, practically into the village of Loos, near " Crucifix Dump ").

The great disadvantage, from the C.O.'s point of view, to the occupation of Duke Street was the fact that it had no accommodation whatsoever, and to aggravate our plight, it rained steadily the whole day and most of the first night. The C.O. lost no time in organising and directing working parties out of the headquarters' staff to construct shelters and dug-outs. Signallers, clerks, orderlies and officers' batmen, under his own personal supervision, worked incessantly all the following day in erecting a new headquarters. On the afternoon of our third day in Duke Street, the vigilant Hun observers must have spotted the activities of our shelter construction parties, and just to remind us there was a war on, they subjected us to a *mauvais quart d'heure*, with salvoes of 5.9's, fired in quick succession. Luckily, we managed to get clear without any casualties, and we were also fortunate in having little or no damage done to our hastily-constructed shelters The staff captain at Brigade Headquarters was tactless enough to ring up the C.O. at this inopportune moment to enquire " if he considered the present ration of sugar issued to the troops could be replaced by half the quantity of jam and part golden syrup." The staff captain may possibly have realised that the question was somewhat untimely by the reply given by Colonel Young, to the effect that he would make it the subject of a "priority" message later in the evening.

The next evening, in Duke Street—incidentally our last one—came the memorable raid by the 7th Leinsters, just south of the Double Crassier. To us, merely spectators, it looked magnificent. The sky was lurid with multi-coloured flares and rockets. The crimson burst of the shrapnel and high explosive rivalled the finest pyrotechnic display that could be imagined. Simultaneously with the announcement of zero by our artillery barrage, dense clouds of gas and smoke were released from our friends the "Loos Wallers." The satisfaction to us watching the gas drifting silently towards the enemy was tremendous. Had we not suffered bitterly but a few weeks back from that same poison ?

To glance back towards the batteries around "Quality Street" was to gaze on lines of stabbing, spitting flames out of the darkness. For an hour the din raged, then gradually subsided in silence back to normal trench warfare.

On the night of the 8th inst. we relieved the 8th Inniskillings in the familiar defence of the left sub-sector (Loos), taking over from English Alley to North Street, with the usual company boundaries.

"A," "B" and "C" Companies occupied the front line, with "D" Company in support (cellars of Pip Street).

Though it was some time since we had held the Loos Sector, the situation was altered very little. The sudden appearance of "Seaforth Crater" on our front made matters a little awkward, and for a few days caused a certain amount of well-founded anxiety to the company commander holding that particular bit of trench. Before we completed our customary tour of four days, Captain V. H. Parr and twenty other ranks did some exceedingly useful and valuable patrol work in the vicinity of the crater. Though the crater had been reported to us on relieving to be unoccupied, the position with regard to it was somewhat obscure. The above-mentioned patrol cleared up the situation satisfactorily, and gave us a clear idea of the enemy's position on the "eastern lip." During the tour, the extreme brightness of the weather, and the consequent clearness of visibility, made the artillery fire on both sides abnormally keen. Second-Lieutenant J. S. Knox and Second-Lieutenant M. Elvery were wounded on the 11th inst.; the former succumbed to his wounds on the following day, and was interred in the battalion cemetery in Philosophe.

On the night of the 12th the battalion was relieved by the

8th Inniskillings, and moved back to Philosophe East into Brigade reserve. " B " Company (Captain R. G. Kerr) remained behind in occupation of the village line and Lens Road Redoubt ; for tactical purposes the company was attached to the front line battalion commander. After four days in reserve, the battalion again took over the line from the 8th Battalion. This was the last time Battalion Headquarters occupied " Fort Innis- killing," which by now was, in our opinion, one of the best and most comfortable " funk holes " along the divisional front. The new signal dug-out, completed a few weeks before, was a great acquisition to the signal communication of the sector. Lieutenant T. D. Ferguson, R.E., the Brigade Signal Officer, kindly lent his assistance in the wiring of the office, and gave much help in the construction of a new trench telephone system in this sector. Retaliation was speeded up considerably as a result.

The following days passed quickly and fairly quietly until we were relieved. The C.O. made daily visits round his companies, inspecting their trenches and ordering improvements in the wire at various points in the line.

It was on one of these ambulatory visits to the front line that a somewhat amusing episode occurred. Dusk had set in, when the C.O., accompanied by the signal officer, had just left the right company headquarters, near North Street. The C.O. thought there was just time to visit a few posts in the front line before dark. As he came to the sentry on duty, at the junction of Seaforth Alley with the front line, he noticed a " dummy " head and shoulders lying on the fire-step. These dummies were issued to entice the enemy snipers to fire at them, whilst one of our picked marksmen was detailed to get the " sniper " from a flank. The C.O. held the figure above the parapet for several minutes, but the Boche took no action. The C.O. was obviously dis- appointed that he could not draw any rifle fire, and calling over to the sentry standing near, he said : " Does the enemy take no notice of these figures ? " The sentry smiled sardonically, and replied in a somewhat offended tone of voice : " Ah, shure, he'll probably fire over a packet of rifle grenades in a few minutes." The C.O. smiled at the repartee, but took the wise precaution of not awaiting their arrival.

On the 19th the battalion was relieved by the 1st Royal Munster Fusiliers, and moved into the huts at Noeux-les-Mines. Owing to the movements of troops down south, and the consequent change of dispositions on the corps front, the 49th Brigade had to relieve a brigade of the 15th Division in the centre and left sub- sectors of the Hulluch Sector. Consequently, on the following night (the 20th) we relieved the 11th Argyle and Sutherland Highlanders in the Hulluch sector. We only remained in this sector for two days, when the 1st R.M.F. side-stepped from Loos, being relieved by a battalion of the 40th Division, and took over from us on the night of the 22nd-23rd.

Once again we marched back to the huts at Noeux, where we remained until the 31st.

A draft of a hundred men and four officers, mostly belonging to the Connaught Rangers, joined us on the 25th as reinforcements, which we badly needed. No less than *twelve new officers joined the battalion during the ensuing week to replace the casualties and those who had been evacuated sick during the past five months of trench warfare.

All the officers who came out with the battalion in February were invited to dinner by the C.O. at Battalion Headquarters on the 27th inst., and the few of us who were still on the strength spent an enjoyable evening at Battalion Headquarters. Unfortunately, many of our old friends were missing.

On the following day the Brigade held their first Horse Show in Noeux. The battalion transport captured many of the most important events, due to the care and efficiency of Second-Lieutenant H. F. Reid and the *personnel* under his charge. The following is a detail of the events won :—

> Officers' Chargers—Lieutenant-Colonel H. N. Young—
> First Prize ; Major A. D. Reid—Second Prize.
> Field Kitchens—First Prize.
> Pack Mules—First Prize.
> G.S Limber Wagons—First Prize.
> Best N.C.O.'s Horse—Sergeant Stafford—First Prize.
> Wagon Driving—Second Prize.
> L.D. Horse—First Prize.

The Divisional Commander congratulated the C.O. on the turn-out and smartness of the drivers and animals. Immediately after the show was over, the Colonel issued orders for a general parade in marching order, and about 6 p.m. the whole battalion, with its first line transport, set out for training under war conditions. The march in the cool of the evening, aided by the strains of the bands, was most pleasant, and provided a change from the monotony of routine life. Leaving the town by the Bethune Road, we turned away to the left across a track towards Vaudricourt, where we rejoined the main road to La Beuvriére. By dusk we arrived at the picturesque and peaceful country near Labuissiere. Here we bivouacked for the night, and companies, under their respective commanders, put out outposts. Early

---

*2/Lieut. W. Hamilton.
2/Lieut. J. A. McCambridge.
2/Lieut. J. R. Moore.
2/Lieut. J. S. Foley.

2/Lieut. H. G. Porter.
2/Lieut. W. T. Smythe.
2/Lieut. T. E. Johnston.
2/Lieut. N. H. Woods.

2/Lieut. J. T. Flanagan.
2/Lieut. C. N. B. Walker.
2/Lieut. J. J. Glenn.
2/Lieut. H. V. Lowry.

the following morning Major-General Hickie and Brigadier-General Leveson Gower inspected the picket line, and expressed satisfaction at the plan of the exercise.

After the inspection the men were allowed to fall out, and for the rest of the day (except for a voluntary church parade given by Father Kelly, which officers and men of all denominations attended) they enjoyed themselves as they liked—sports, reading and sleeping were indulged in. Everyone enjoyed themselves to the full, and felt quite sorry to have to return in the evening to the routine and boredom of Noeux.

At 6 p.m. the battalion marched back to billets, and the following day saw them once again at the greatest game of all. On the 31st we relieved the 7th Leinsters in Philosophe West.

Captain A. C. Taggart, the Adjutant, was evacuated sick to No. 1 C.C.S., from whence he was subsequently sent home. He rejoined us again after six months. Captain D. H. Morton took over his duties for a few weeks, with effect from the 1st August, and later handed over to Second-Lieutenant J. A. Foley on the 26th August.

On the 4th inst. the battalion relieved the 8th Inniskillings at Puits 14 bis, and after the usual period was relieved by the 8th R.D.F., and moved into Brigade support. Tenth Avenue was always the object of improvement, and this tour was no exception. Great activity was directed by the C.O. on completing the new Battalion Headquarters which the tunnellers had commenced off " Northern Up." As usual, the Colonel directed the operations personally, and many officers and " callers " at Battalion Headquarters during those days found themselves snared for a " job of work." Countless sand-bags were filled from early morning until dark, and at the end of our four days the work was well on the way to completion. On the 12th we took over the front line again until the 16th, when we moved back to the huts in Mazingarbe.

Major Ross White and Captain J. Ritty, M.C., rejoined us from England on the 15th ; the former was given temporary employment on Brigade Headquarters staff, and the latter took over command of " C " Company from Lieutenant Lefevre.

The night of the 20th the battalion moved into the line at Loos for the last time. On the 24th the divisional artillery fired off their surplus ammunition as a farewell present from Ireland before going down south, and on the 25th of August we were relieved by the 8th East Lancashire Regiment, and proceeded to Noeux. A draft of a hundred men arrived the same day as reinforcements, mostly from other Irish regiments.

*   *   *   *   *   *

Six months had passed over, practically to a day, since we

first landed in the country. Many new faces had appeared since then, and many of the best we should never see with us again. Yet the spirit of " The Seventh " was still indomitable. The ideal of being " second to none " had survived the monotony and tedium of trench warfare. Through those months of winter and summer we gained our experience and learnt by contact with realities the meaning of the boredom of position warfare— the interminable boredom and the incessant work and detail connected with it. The similarity of our environments ; the going in and coming out of the same trenches time after time ; the everlasting lines of chalk ; the dark and cold of the long winter nights ; the never-ending fatigue parties and trench duties ; the discipline of work and of sleep—all must remain indelibly stamped on our memories of the Loos Salient in 1916. Lieutenant M. J. Daly sums up the situation in his never-to-be-forgotten adage : " Indent and Salve."

The Commander-in-Chief, Field-Marshal Sir Douglas Haig, in his despatch dated 19th May, 1916, with reference to the winter campaign of 1916 says :—" The maintenance and repair of our " defences alone, especially in winter, entails constant and heavy " work. Bad weather and the enemy combine to flood and destroy " trenches, dug-outs and communications ; all such damages must " be repaired promptly, under fire, and almost entirely by night." In the same despatch he says : " While many other units " have done excellent work during the period under review, the " following have been specially brought to my notice for good " work in carrying out or repelling local attacks and raids : " .   .   .   The 7th (" S ") Battalion Royal Inniskilling " Fusiliers. .   . "

The only remembrance we could leave behind us was the little cemetery behind the bakery at Philosophe East. In that field was an acre of ground, hallowed by the battalion ; it was the everlasting record of those who had made the supreme sacrifice.

In a larger sense we cannot dedicate, we cannot consecrate, we cannot hallow that ground. The brave men, living and dead, who struggled there, have consecrated it far above our power to add or detract. The world will little note, nor long remember, what we say here, but it never can forget what they did there. It is for us, the living, rather to be dedicated here to the unfinished work which they who fought there have thus far so nobly advanced. It is rather for us to be here dedicated to the great task remaining before us ; that from these honoured dead we take increased devotion to that cause for which they gave the last full measure of devotion ; that we here highly resolve that these dead shall not have died in vain.

CHAPTER V.

THE BATTLE OF THE SOMME, 1916.

Leaving the Loos Salient—Lapugnoy—The journey south—Detraining at Longneau—The march to Vaux-sur-Somme—Gibraltar Camp, The Citadel and Billon Farm—Moving up the Line—Maricourt—Relieving the 12th Rifle Brigade—Guillemont—Support in Bernafay Wood—The Battle of Ginchy—The relief by the Guards on September 10th, 1916—Our casualties—Major Weldon takes command—Leaving the battle area—An appreciation by General Ludendorff of the fighting.

On the 26th August, 1916, at 11 a.m., the battalion " fell-in " near the huts at Noeux-les-Mines and proceeded, *via* Vaudricourt and Bruay, to Lapugnoy. Although the day was hot and sultry, and the men were undoubtedly tired after their long march from Loos the night before, not a single man fell out on the line of march. For the first time for many months our transport and quartermaster's department accompanied us, as, of course, up to this they only had local movements through the billeting areas of the Loos Sector.

Obviously, our ultimate destination was the " Somme," but at the time (though rumour was always current about likely movements) nobody, not even the C.O., knew. The secret was so well preserved by the Staff that to our amazement the civilian inhabitants of Lapugnoy assured us that we were bound for Amiens and the Somme !

Lapugnoy afforded us three days of the most pleasant and refreshing rest. After the past few months of continual trenches and fatigues, our new billets seemed a veritable paradise. Billets were clean and unmolested from shell fire, and, to crown everything, the weather was perfect. The 7th Royal Irish Fusiliers were also billeted in the village, but this did not form any inconvenience or overcrowding in the billeting arrangements, which were adequate for the necessities of both battalions. Our three days' rest was employed, for the most part, in cleaning and refitting. The men received baths and clean changes of clothing, and by the second day, "spit and polish" reigned supreme. In anticipation of an early departure, the C.O., in the course of several lectures, discussed the many details connected with semi-open warfare and the usual precautions to take under the different situations that might arise. He seemed convinced from his manner that our share in the Great Push would be to break the toughest part of the Hun line (a conviction which was not altogether unfounded, as later events showed), so that he gave us detailed instructions on what he termed "how to dig ourselves in for good." The expression caused the officers to be anxiously amused. As the conference dispersed, one company commander was heard to advise his subalterns : "According to the predictions of the C.O., as far as I can see, everyone of you will receive a cross ; whether it's a wooden or a silver one depends on your own individual luck."—C'est la guerre.

Shortly after daybreak on the 29th inst. the battalion moved off, after a somewhat busy night spent in packing and loading up our stores and ammunition on the limbers. Our local destination was the entraining station of Fouqueroil, which we reached after about an hour's march. Advantage was taken at the station, on our arrival, to provide the troops with breakfast, which had been cooking en route. The 'modus operandi' at the entraining station was the usual one connected with operations of the kind—everyone got cursed for something—it didn't really matter who he was or what he was doing. "Here, you, lift a hand to this blood-stained box, will you ? " or " Detail a party there to help those ' b——' cookers up the ramp," etc., etc. It must not be imagined, because of these little expressions of "affection," that there was any confusion—on the contrary, the boxing of the animals was finished in a remarkably short period. The fact that the railway trucks were too small to meet the requirements of the G.S. wagons was, perhaps, the cause of some well-founded anxiety to the C.O. and the transport officer (Second-Lieutenant H. F. Reid). The difficulty was overcome, however, by having them lifted bodily on to the trucks.

The train was only an hour late in starting, which was remarkably good for this part of the country. Slowly, but surely, it rattled on towards Amiens, *via* St. Pol. During the railway journey we witnessed the novel and unusual spectacle of a complete New Zealand division on the line of march, stretching for miles along the roads. Time after time we crossed and re-crossed them during the journey (obviously they were also bound for the Battle of the Somme). A violent thunderstorm broke during the afternoon, and developed into a wet evening, which looked none too rosy for our detrainment and the inevitable trek to our new billeting area.

About 5 p.m. we passed through Amiens Station, and half an hour later we pulled into the military siding (for it was nothing more) at Longneau. Here we detrained in about twenty minutes, and within a few moments were clear of the station, en route for billets somewhere in the neighbourhood of Corbie. The rain and mud of the roads made it a most cheerless and tiresome march. Our one hope was that our billets were not far away; this was not to be, they were much further than we had imagined.

The rain having ceased about 7 p.m., we halted and made tea at the side of the road. This did much to improve our spirits ; it was our first meal since breakfast that morning. After tea, and about an hour's halt, we continued our march. French troops passed us on the road, and by way of greeting gave us a quaint version of " Tipperary," which afforded us much amusement, and brought back the memories of a comfortable fire and bed—it seemed years ago since we had been at Tipperary ; in reality, not so very long.

By 7-30 p.m. the dusk had given place to the inky darkness of a damp and dreary night. It was not till about 9-30 p.m. we clattered over the rough *pavé* of Corbie, and on the initiative of the R.S.M., who was at the head of column, we struck up a song. " How much further ? " was the question. Yet nobody knew. Some had hopes that our destination might be Corbie itself—they were wrong. The C.O. urged us that it was only another mile—" certainly it wasn't more than five." By 11-30 p.m. we arrived at Vaux-sur-Somme, and though the rain had now ceased some considerable time, yet the night was so pitch dark that it was only with difficulty, and after much excusable delay, we could get the battalion into billets. By 1 a.m. we were asleep, tired out. Captain D. H. Morton was unfortunately suffering from a very high fever and had to leave us for hospital on the following morning. The village of Vaux-sur-Somme was small, inhabited by farming peasants ; it was dirty, enclosed by a belt of trees, and had the outward appearance of poverty and sleepiness.

On the 31st we advanced a stage nearer the battle, and it proved to be a most interesting march along the main Amiens-Bray Road, and down into Happy Valley. What a host of memories and associations must ever be connected with Happy Valley ! Dotted about with transport lines, observation balloon sections, divisional headquarters, with here and there enormous dumps of ammunition, R.E. material and ordnance stores ; it was, apparently, the supply area of the front, and at that time was comparatively immune from hostile shell fire. Through the middle of this motley assortment of tents, bivouacs and horse lines, we found our way up to Gibraltar Camp. On the outskirts of the camp we had the pleasure of seeing His Royal Highness the Prince of Wales.

On reaching the camp we soon discovered that the tent accommodation provided was not going to be sufficient for the battalion. This was of little or no consequence, as the weather was so hot that it was preferable to sleep in the open. The greatest disadvantage of our new home was the existence of what one might almost describe as a plague of flies. These insects caused us such annoyance that we organised a campaign for their extermination—the measures adopted were of little or no avail.

Bathing parades in the Somme (just south of Bray) afforded most delightful recreation after the hot and dusty march all day. The following evening an impromptu smoking concert was organised by the C.O. in a field beside the camp. In spite of the fact that there was no piano to assist us in our musical numbers, everyone enjoyed it immensely. Private Knight was the *pièce de resistance* in his humorous song entitled " The Clothes Horse." The refrain of this comic song suggested that the only horse that he would care to ride upon was the one the missus dried the clothes on !

The following day the Brigadier, in the course of a short lecture, gave us a rough outline and some important information regarding the portion of line we should have to take over ; he also gave us a general *resumé* of the likely forthcoming operations. On the morning of the 3rd September, shortly after 9 o'clock we advanced a further stage towards the battle line ; this time quite a short distance away, to a camp known as " The Citadel," so called, evidently, because of its position on the top of the hill. The accommodation was certainly a great improvement on the " Happy Valley," and by mid-day the whole battalion was comfortably fixed up in the new camp.

All day we were under orders to move at short notice.

During the afternoon we awaited news of the attack, which the artillery barrage told us was in progress in front. For miles around the battle area was bedecked with our observation balloons. The terrific violence of the gun-fire during the day had by now increased to drum fire, and it was commonly supposed that the attack on Guillemont had been launched.

Orders were received late in the evening that we were moving to bivouacs about a mile further forward, and by 11 o'clock, after a short, but highly disagreeable, march across derelict trenches and the remains of a belt of what had once been formidable barbed wire, we arrived at our new camping area. What luxury awaited us ! Two tents, in a very small field unsheltered on all sides from the elements. Our location was now " Billon Farm," though the farm really only existed on the map. Rain began to fall before the men had time to erect bivouacs out of their ground sheets, and altogether the night was not a pleasant one. The first arrivals were the luckiest ; they found some pieces of sheet iron and empty ammunition boxes, which afforded some shelter from the weather. Towards morning the rain ceased, and a bitter north-easterly breeze sprang up which made it impossible to sleep, as we were exposed to it from all sides. The next day the colonel and company commanders went up to reconnoitre the district we had been ordered to take over.

. Being under orders to move at an hour's notice, arrangements were made for detailing " B " echelon (a nucleus of men left out of the line) and for the transport and quartermaster's staff. Billon Farm from then became our " Rear Headquarters."

At 7 p.m. the battalion moved up to take over the line, with Major Reid at the head. During the preliminary stages of the march we passed an endless stream of ambulances returning from the line. The roads were *choc-à-bloc* in places with transport carts, ammunition limbers and staff cars. The battalion kept to the tracks wherever it could. Eventually we arrived within the battery zone around Maricourt.

Maricourt depicted a scene of the utmost desolation and ruin ; shapeless and shell-shattered houses were all that remained of what was once, no doubt, a prosperous village. French gunners and infantry inhabiting the cellars stood at their doors and exchanged greetings with us as we passed. Everywhere there was activity : rations being brought up under cover of night ; ammunition to the guns ; material for consolidating the new lines ; ambulances continually passing with the wounded from the front. Incidentally, Maricourt was the dividing line between the British and French troops at this time.

Evening drew on. On through Maricourt towards the Briqueterie we passed batteries of all calibres, blazing away continuously. By the time we came to the Briqueterie it was ten o'clock, and the rain had increased to a steady downpour. Here the C.O. and company officers met us to guide us over the shell-swept area to our position. It would be impossible to describe our subsequent progress through the mud and water-logged shell holes ; past Bernafay Wood, Trones Wood and up to Arrow Head Copse. The journey was slow and interminable, through the medley of battered and disused trenches, which had been the scenes of much of the heavy fighting during the previous weeks. Fortunately, the enemy's artillery was inactive ; only once we happened to come in for a few salvoes of high-bursting

E

shrapnel, and an occasional 5.9, some sixty to a hundred yards on our flank. By 2 a.m. we reached Arrow Head Copse and the battlefields of the fighting which had taken place a day or two previously. Here we beheld for the first time the awful and ghastly spectacle of an uncleared battlefield—absolute chaos and utter desolation everywhere. Shapeless masses of human beings lay strewn over the ground. The very air reeked with the smell of putrefying flesh and blood.

Occasionally the flares in front would show up the grim horror of it all, then dwindle and die out, leaving us to pick our way through the abandoned material as best we could. Friend and enemy were the same there. Broken rifles, ammunition boxes, equipment, all bore testimony of the terrible wastage of war. Still we plodded on through the mud and stench. Fortunately, the rain cleared away about 3 a.m. Even this had but little effect on the " going," as the shell holes by now were water-logged.

Certainly, it was the most cheerless night we had yet experienced for a relief. To add to our discomfort, the guides were uncertain as to the way ; in fact, looking back over it all, it almost seems a mystery how we arrived in Guillemont as soon as we did.

By 3-30 a.m. we were on the outskirts of the village—at least, we were according to the map. In the murky light of dawn we could just distinguish where the village had been. There was nothing of it to be seen but a heap of crumbled and distorted masonry. It is difficult to describe such a scene of absolute wanton desolation. The whole area was nothing more or less than a wilderness of shell holes.

We crossed a sunken road about 200 yards to the south of the village, and then made a detour round the village from the west. The morning was hazy and, consequently, visibility was low, otherwise there might have been a different tale to tell. Luckily, the enemy left us alone to proceed to the line and take over. By 5-30 a.m. we had relieved what was left of the 12th Rifle Brigade. Almost twelve hours had elapsed since we had set out from Billon Farm the previous evening.

The C.O. supervised the relief, and by 6-30 a.m. the Coy's were disposed, and holding a line as follows :—

" A " Company (Captain V. H. Parr). The west side of Leuze Wood. (The position in the wood itself seemed somewhat obscure.)

" B " Company (Captain R. G. Kerr) and " D " Company (Captain Stainforth) were situated in a shell-crater position along the Ginchy-Wedge Wood Road. (T.26a and c.)

" C " Company (Captain J. Ritty, M.C.) on the Guillemont-Leuze Wood Road. (T.20 b.)

Battalion Headquarters in a derelict enemy shelter south of Guillemont village. (About T.25 b.)

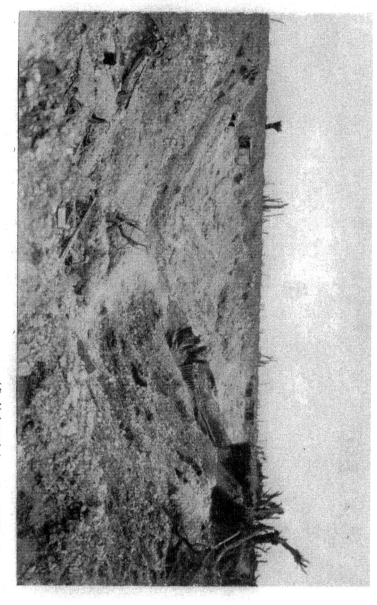

GUILLEMONT VILLAGE—SOMME, 1916. (By kind permission of Imperial War Museum.)

The relief had been carried out, at any rate, without any casualties, but the enemy made up in this respect before the day was over. The companies worked as hard as possible throughout the day improving the line, putting it in a state of defence, and making every endeavour to link up the isolated posts. The day cleared up about noon, and with this came the advent of the hostile activity. Spasmodically throughout the day the Hun dosed us with whizz-bangs and 5.9's. Intermittent bursts of fire were directed on the ruins of Guillemont village, the cemetery to the east, and the south-west corner of Leuze Wood. By 4 o'clock in the afternoon the hostile shelling became more consistent. Fire was concentrated on the Ginchy-Wedge Wood Road, and some casualties were sustained in consequence in " B " and " D " Companies. About this time Captain C. H. Stainforth was wounded in the leg, and Second-Lieutenant C. A. Crowe took over command of his company.

During the night " A " Company took advantage of the darkness and improved their position in the wood. They pushed out patrols and ascertained the craters occupied by the enemy. Second-Lieutenant W. T. Smythe and Lieutenant Ruddock did some very good patrol work in connection with this enterprise.

The night passed quietly, which enabled the rations to be got up in safety. The transport wagons were able to come nearly as far as Maltz Horn Farm, though they were severely hampered by the heavy state of the roads. Not only this, but the fact that ammunition was brought to the guns at night, made battalion first line transport very difficult in the forward zone.

The following day (the 6th) opened under unfavourable auspices for the battalion. The C.O., whilst visiting the line occupied by Captain R. G. Kerr and his company, was severely wounded by a sniper. The loss of Colonel H. N. Young at such a critical time, and in view of impending operations, was a great blow to the unit. So badly had he been hit that we feared he would never recover from his wound. He was evacuated, as quickly as possible under the existing conditions, and sent down the line, and eventually to England. (He recovered after some little time, and was able to come back and command the battalion in 1917). Major A. D. Reid, who had come up to visit us the night before from " B " echelon, was on the spot, and assumed command of the battalion.

During the day (for the visibility was good) the enemy was particularly active with his artillery. Possibly, it was merely retaliation for our merciless and continuous bombardments of his defences, but it looked like registration fire, as a forerunner to counter-attack. Leuze Wood and the Guillemont vicinity received most attention.

By nightfall we were to learn the method of the Hun madness.

Shortly before 8 p.m. (as it was getting dusk) a hurricane bombardment descended over the whole battalion area. " A " Company (Captain Parr) was submitted to concentrated fire of the most intense nature. Machine-guns played on their flank from the direction of Ginchy Telegraph.

Under cover of this sweeping barrage the Boche attempted to regain a footing in the wood, but was unsuccessful. Captain V. H. Parr and his company repulsed the attack all along the wood, and held all the ground they had won the night before.

Our artillery, when they saw the S.O.S. rockets, put down a most effective barrage on the enemy's lines, and the heavies presumably were employed on counter-battery. The whole attack only lasted forty-five minutes. The position after the attack was that we were in possession of the entire wood, with posts established on the reverse slope to the east.

Supports were never called for, though Major Reid imagined at one time he might have to send up a company to reinforce the right flank, which looked like being left " in the air." When the situation became normal once again the O.C. ordered " B " and " D " Companies forward to the south and south-west boundaries of the wood, in closer support, lest the Boche would renew the attack at dawn. Simultaneously with this movement he moved his headquarters to that evacuated by " D " Company.

In consideration of the intensity of the barrage, our casualties were remarkably slight. " A " Company suffered about twenty-five in all—mostly wounded. Captain Parr was wounded during the attack, but remained at duty.

On the following morning Major A. D. Reid, R.S.M. Dolan and three of headquarters' *personnel* were wounded by the same shell. Considering the loss of Colonel Young only the day before, this came as a most unfortunate blow. The acting-adjutant (Second-Lieutenant J. Foley) and the signal officer (Lieutenant G. A. C. Walker) were now the only two officers left at headquarters ; the former was suffering from a severe attack of trench fever which rendered him almost ineffective. Captain R. G. Kerr (" B " Company) was sent for, and took over command of the battalion. Lieutenant A. E. C. Trimble assumed command of his company.

During the day there was unusual activity on the part of the enemy, though our aircraft and artillery worked unceasingly throughout the day in preparation for the next great attack on the Hun. This time we understood the objective would be Ginchy.

At 7 o'clock that night (the 7th inst.) the battalion was relieved by the 4th Battalion London Regiment. After the relief, companies moved independently to Bernafay Wood, where the Brigade was concentrated in divisional support. It was 10 p.m. before the whole battalion arrived in the wood, but within a short time after arrival the men took advantage of their position for a well-earned rest. It was the first opportunity we had, since coming into the battle zone, to sleep undisturbed. Some derelict trenches and shelters still existed in the wood, and the most was made of these to make ourselves as comfortable as possible under the circumstances. On arrival the Transport Officer awaited us with the rations and, more important, a good issue of rum. Despite the continuous roar of some six-inch howitzers in the vicinity of our bivouacs, all ranks slept soundly throughout the night, thoroughly exhausted after the previous few days.

Orders came through on the morning of the 8th that we should proceed to Guillemont that night and take up a position east of the village, ready to support the attack on Ginchy village at a time which would be notified us later. The C.O. held a conference of company commanders and senior N.C.O.'s during the morning, and read over the operation orders. He ordered one officer from each company to go up to the village in daylight and reconnoitre the locality where their company would take up its position. Having done so, they would return to the battalion and act as guides for their own companies.

By 7 p.m. companies had started to move forward independently of one another along the Montauban-Guillemont Road. The approach to the village along this road was much more favourable than moving across the open ground around Arrow Head Copse. At any rate, we could keep our direction, which was more than could easily be done at night over a desert of shell holes. Leaving Trones Wood on the left of the road, we approached the village through the quarries. Here the 7th Royal Irish Fusiliers were already getting into their position for the great attack.

Companies, with the aid of their own guides, were not long in locating their positions, and shortly after arrival at their places of assembly, they commenced to link up the shell holes and get under cover before dawn. Advice of their arrival and the positions taken up by them was duly reported to the C.O., who by now had taken over the Battalion Headquarters of the 11th Hants. Regiment in the sunken road 100 yards east of Guillemont (T. 19 D.), locally known as " Mount Street." The dispositions of the companies at this time were as follows :—

" A " Company (Lieutenant Ruddock) along " Brompton Road " (north-west of the village).

" B " Company (Lieutenant Trimble) between " Brompton Road " and " Green Street," behind " A " Company.

"C" Company (Captain Ritty) from "Mount Street" to junction of "North Street" and "Green Street."

"D" Company (Second-Lieutenant Crowe) from Ginchy-Guillemont Road to "Mount Street."

The night of the 8th-9th was comparatively quiet, and unattended with casualties. Desultory machine-gun fire was directed on different points of the village, otherwise it was a very favourable night for linking up the shell holes to form cover for the brigade and getting under cover. The 49th Brigade was in support to the 47th and 48th Brigades, who were "going over" first in the attack on Ginchy next day. The 8th Royal Inniskilling Fusiliers and ourselves formed the support to the right flank of the attack (the 47th Infantry Brigade). Early on the morning of the 9th the Commanding Officer of the 8th Battalion, Colonel Dalziel Walton, was killed by a sniper close to our headquarters. His loss was most deeply regretted by the whole brigade.

Before dawn on the 9th inst. our artillery was active, and kept up a slow barrage fire on the enemy's defences during the morning. The Boche replied consistently, but without any appreciable effect, probably due to the poor visibility during the early hours of the morning and the determination of our air craft to keep his sausage balloons downstairs.

Instructions were received during the morning that the battalion was to get in touch with the C.O. 6th Royal Irish Regiment, under whose orders we were to act after "zero."

Zero was fixed at 4-45 o'clock in the afternoon, and promptly at the appointed hour a bombardment of terrific intensity opened out from our guns. The Hun replied for the most part with shrapnel, and with the most deadly machine-gun fire from the direction of Ginchy Telegraph. The 48th Brigade succeeded in penetrating through the village, and beyond, but the 47th Brigade, whom we were supporting, were temporarily held up by machine-gun fire, and they suffered very heavy casualties.

The battalion was quickly moved forward to support the right under most unfavourable auspices—the enemy were by now barraging the approaches and tracks through Guillemont with great intensity.

Advancing over the open ground east of the village, the companies—more especially "C" and "D"—came under the most intense machine-gun and rifle fire. For a time, it seemed as though the battalion would be decimated, as the line of advancing platoons was swept from end to end with a hail of bullets. To add to this, the enemy had put down a most effective shrapnel barrage behind the British front line.

About 5-30 p.m. Ginchy had fallen to the Left Brigade; in

fact, the enemy was so completely demoralised by the initial stages of the attack that his defences were now totally disorganised in the village of Ginchy. The fact that the Left Brigade had captured their objective, however, did not in any way ease the situation for us on the right, where the enemy's line was still practically intact, supported by numerous machine-guns which had evidently escaped our creeping barrage. Considering that the Right Brigade had suffered so heavily, it was quite impossible to expect us, as supporting battalion to the right flank, to restore the situation, and make a fresh effort. Our own casualties getting to the front line over the open were sufficient to cancel any such hope being entertained.

The only policy to adopt under the circumstances was to hold on, and at all costs stop the enemy if he counter-attacked from the flank, thereby attempting to cut off the salient made by the advancing troops on Ginchy. Even this task was a difficult proposition at our reduced strength. Obviously, the only hope the enemy had of regaining lost ground was to strike now, before we had time to reorganise our line. His attack, however, when it did come, was broken up and no ground was lost.

Back in Guillemont the scene was one of great activity and excitement. Of course, the Hun made desperate efforts by his barrage fire to stop reserves being sent up to exploit the success. The shelling was unpleasant, as artillery fire always was, but no serious inconvenience was caused by this action. Batches of prisoners were now coming down from Ginchy with their escorts, and a continual procession of walking wounded made their way to the aid posts at the Quarry. The proportion of slightly wounded in this action was greater than one would have expected under the circumstances.

By 6 p.m. the C.O. was able to speak to the Brigadier on the telephone, and give him some details of the attack and a general outline of the situation. A definite appreciation was impossible at that time owing to the position on the right being still obscure.

Second-Lieutenant H. B. O. Mitchell, M.C., the battalion Lewis gun officer, ascertained some useful information later in the evening.

Before nightfall the enemy attempted another counter-attack, which was successfully repulsed by the remnants of three battalions, ourselves included. A continuous and most destructive barrage was maintained by the enemy almost until midnight, and our casualties were heavy. No less than two company commanders were killed, Captain J. Ritty, M.C., and Second-Lieutenant A. C. Crowe (" D " Company) ; Second-Lieutenant T. R. Moore, Second-Lieutenant W. Morgan, and Second-Lieutenant H. Maguire were also killed in the attack.

The total casualties for the battle were five officers and 184 other ranks.

About 2 o'clock on the morning of the 10th inst. the Guards had relieved the 16th Division, and the battalion "crawled" back to Billon Farm by easy stages, arriving at about 9 o'clock. Lieutenant Ruddock, with what remained of " A " Company, met the C.O. in Maricourt, and enjoyed a smoke by the side of the road—a most welcome halt in the long trek back to camp.

The quartermaster had made arrangements for a good break-fast when the men arrived, which they enjoyed prior to a good long rest for the remainder of the day. In the afternoon Major K. C. Weldon, Royal Dublin Fusiliers, took over command of the battalion, and Captain R. G. Kerr became second-in-command from that date.

On the 11th inst. the battalion moved by route march to billets at Sailly-le-Sec, bidding farewell to the battlefields of the Somme for many a long day to come.

* * * * * *

To relate in greater detail the procession of events which happened to us during our short visit to the Somme area would be impossible without taking up more than the allotted space, and it would also entail matters relating to military tactics, which might invoke individual criticisms.

Only the main outlines of our experiences have been related.

The temporary loss of our gallant commanding officer, our second-in-command (Major Reid) and several of our company commanders had, undoubtedly, a great effect on our capabilities as a whole.

Many of our best officers and men, who had so worthily upheld the traditions of "The Seventh," and maintained the spirit of the regiment, now lay on the battlefields of the Somme. The fact that the 16th Division had done its part so well in the battle, and that we were able to share its honour, made us proud of those we left behind. It was our first serious taste of war. Nothing hitherto could have been compared to it.

It is interesting in reading the " War Memories " of General Ludendorff to learn that the fall of Ginchy meant so much to the enemy. Speaking of the battles fought during September, 1916, he says :—" The battles that were then fought are amongst " the most fiercely contested of the whole war, and far exceeded " all previous offensives as regards the number of men and the " amount of material employed.

" North of the Somme the attack was resumed as early as " the 3rd September, and lasted until the 7th. The enemy " penetrated into our positions more and more deeply. On

" September 5th, south of the Somme, the French also attacked
" on a wide front, and gained ground at several points. On
" the northern bank, fighting began on the 9th and lasted until
" the 17th. We were thrown back still further. Ginchy and
" Bouchavesnes fell into the enemy's hands. . . . Great
" were our losses."

To a large extent the opinion of the enemy Chief of Staff is
shared by those who took part in the engagements in the great
Battle of the Somme of 1916. It was a battle of extermination—
neither side yielded ground without doing so at a most tremendous
price. No amount of shell fire, ammunition, material or sacrifice
was spared to gain an objective, and above all to inflict casualties
on the enemy.

To our own higher command the capture of Ginchy, Guillemont
and Leuze Wood were very important factors at the time, for it
was by gaining these positions that the attack of September 15th
became possible, and the ultimate retreat of the enemy to the
Hindenburg line.

The messages quoted below, received from the numerous General
Officers over us, bear ample testimony of the importance of our
success :—

The Corps Commander says : " I heartily congratulate the
" G.O.C. and all ranks of the 16th (Irish) Division on their capture
" of Ginchy, which, following on the capture of Guillemont, adds
" fresh laurels to those already gained. The gallantry and devotion
" of all ranks during these recent operations has been beyond all
" praise."

The South African Brigade wired to the 16th Division :—
" Hearty congratulations on your success."

" The G.O.C., 49th Infantry Brigade, wishes to express his
" admiration for the conduct and gallantry of all ranks of the
" 49th Infantry Brigade during the recent operations, during
" which they have added greatly to the honour of their regiments
" and corps, and also their country. The discipline displayed
" and the bravery exhibited was most marked."

CHAPTER VI.

FLANDERS, 1916-1917.

Sailly-le-Sec—The bus journey to Bailleul (near Abbeville)—A short rest and departure north—Detraining at Bailleul (Nord)—Berthen—Relieving the Canadians in Spanbroekmolen Sector—Brigade support in Kemmel—Preparing for the winter—Locre—A dummy raid—Major W. E. Rothwell takes command—Christmas Day in the line—The New Year's honour list—The raid of the 12th January, 1917—Lieutenant-Colonel H. N. Young, D.S.O., rejoins and assumes command—Recreations at Curragh Camp—The " Green and Buffs "—St. Patrick's Day—Recipients of Irish Brigade Certificates for gallantry in the field—A quiet tour in the line—Back in Clare Camp.

Marching back from Billon Farm to Sailly-le-Sec, the battalion was ordered to keep to the tracks across country as much as possible ; this was done in order to keep the main roads clear for the fresh divisions coming down into the battle area, and also to prevent the roads getting blocked up with unnecessary traffic. Most of the main roads in the back areas were *choc-à-bloc* with transport of every description passing to and from the line all day and all night.

About 5 p.m. we arrived at our new billeting area, where we found there was ample accommodation for all. Had the battalion been up to the same strength as when we came down from the Loos Salient, the job of getting the men fixed up comfortably would have been otherwise.

Like most of the country villages near a battle zone—more especially on the Somme—there was very little to do when off duty, and killing time was dull and tiresome. The great comfort on these occasions was to think how much worse off we might have been, and had been before. Vaux-sur-Somme was much more uncomfortable and dirty than our present billets.

Very little work was done by the men whilst we were in Sailly. After all, we considered that we had earned a rest, and the motto was, " Why not take it ? " One never knew what moment we might get shifted either back to the line or off to some other part of the front. The work of reorganising the companies and platoons was sufficient in itself to keep the officers and N.C.O.'s busy. Deficiencies in our equipment and stores had to be made good, and more important at the moment was the state of the men's clothes after the past ten days of mud and shell holes up the line.

Members of the General Staff paid us visits during these days, mostly to congratulate the battalion on their good work, and the Brigade Commander called on the C.O. several times to discuss matters and talk over the future plans of the brigade.

Our next move was on the 18th September, when the whole brigade moved back from the Somme area by bus. Never before had we seen such a convoy of motor buses. It was quite a welcome change to know that we hadn't got to march to some entraining station, for by this time we had our experiences of railway transport on the Western Front ; it was the acme of discomfort and boredom.

Unfortunately, the rain came down fairly heavily before starting, otherwise the journey would have been quite pleasant. As it was, it was quite interesting going through Amiens, though sitting inside a bus when soaked through does not help one to enjoy the surroundings.

It was not until after dark (9 p.m.) that we came to a halt, and the order was passed along from the front that we were to dismount and march to billets. Bailleul, near Abbeville, was our destination, and it was only about fifteen minutes' walk. With the exception of " B " Company, who got held up by some traffic at the rear of the column, we arrived in billets in good time, and in less than an hour most of us were asleep.

Bailleul was one of the most picturesque villages that it was our good fortune to stop at in our peregrinations up to this, and the few nights we spent there were appreciated by all ranks. Perhaps the transport lines were not so lucky. They had only bivouacs on their picket lines, and the rain and mud caused them some discomfort. By this time they were used to swamp and morass, so, bar the usual amount of grousing—which is the privilege of the best soldiers—they made the best of their lot.

For the time being a rest was the only thing we required, and, short as it was, we enjoyed it to the full. The local inhabitants were delighted to see us, which was unusual. They told us they had had no troops billeted there for many months, and seemed only too pleased to help us in any way they could.

The night of the 20th September saw us on the road to the entraining station bound for the usual " unknown destination " somewhere *au nord*. This time, for a change, we had a very short march to the railway, and had little or no trouble in getting loaded up and on the train. The train pulled out shortly after 10 o'clock.

By 9 o'clock the following morning we steamed into Haze-brouck, where the train made a halt for quite a considerable time. Many of the officers repaired to the buffet for a cup of coffee, and during their absence the train moved quietly out of the station, leaving them behind. In a few minutes they discovered what had happened, and after a most exciting race they all caught up and boarded the train. The second-in-command (Major R. G. Kerr) was seen hanging on " by his teeth " to the last carriage, where he had to remain until the train came to the next halt. It was only twenty minutes' ride, and he stuck it out, much to the amusement of the spectators from the windows.

It was 11 a.m. when the battalion detrained at Bailleul (Pas de Calais)—quite a coincidence that the end of our journey should be the same name as our entraining point.

Within an hour we were marching through the town on the way to our new billeting area, which lay in the direction of Mont des Cats. Marching up through the Grande Place of Bailleul the town looked a most peaceful and prosperous place. Were it not for the signal wires, latticed from house to house ; an occasional flag to denote some headquarters ; a few staff cars and mess carts in the square, and a various assortment of troops, Colonial and British, it might have been miles and miles from the firing line. In those days it was almost untouched by shell fire ; to-day it lies a heap of bricks and ruins.

Leaving the Town Hall on the left, we marched down the St. Jean Cappel Road, through St. Jean Cappel, and on to the Berthen area, where we were billeted in scattered farm-houses on the outskirts of the village. This village was in France, but only a mile from the Belgian frontier.

Here, again, the inhabitants informed us that no troops had been billeted in the vicinity for some time, with the result that our reception was once more most welcome, and every comfort afforded us. Some of us fostered the hope that we should remain in this area, but prophecies of this description were never to be relied on in the field.

On the afternoon of the 22nd we got orders that we were moving up the line the next day, and we did.

After an early start on the 23rd September, we marched up, via Locre and Kemmel, to the Spanbroekmolen Sector (about 2,000 yards due east of Kemmel Hill) and relieved the 33rd Canadian Infantry. It was a daylight relief. " A " and " B " Companies took over the front line, with " C " and " D " Companies in reserve, in a position locally referred to as Regent Street dug-outs. Battalion headquarters were some distance behind

CAPT. W. RUDDOCK FRONT
LIEUT. M. ELVERY LINE. 1916.

"FATHER KELLY"

MAJOR V. H. PARR. D.S.O., M.C.
LIEUT. H. F. REID.

Cᵒ H.Q. REGENT ST.
DEC. 1916.

(1,700 yards) in a broken-down farm-house known as Fort Victoria.

The first impressions of our new front—more especially after the desolation of the Somme area—was one of comparative peace and quietness. For the next few months, with a few exceptions, this impression remained. To all intents and purposes there was *nothing doing*—it was typical stagnation trench warfare at its worst.

There was one thing obvious about the sector, and that was that it was a fool's paradise. Should the enemy contemplate a raid or try to worry us with artillery fire, his task was easy, and our position would be most uncomfortable. Another serious disadvantage to the area was the absence of proper dug-outs, or even shelters, to provide protection, and, above all, the drainage question was acute. In wet weather it looked as though we should get flooded out. At the time we took over, the dry season of summer had left the trenches in a fair condition, but this state of luxury did not last long when the weather broke. Before our first tour in the line was over, plans were submitted by the C.O. to the brigade office for two new company headquarters and various other improvements. The main C.T. from the reserve to the front line was little more than a duck-board track for the last two hundred yards. It took several months before Pall Mall (C.T.) was in a reasonable state of repair.

The best news at this time was the re-opening of leave to the United Kingdom. Though the vacancies allotted to the battalion were small, yet the mere fact of getting away sometime bucked everyone up tremendously.

On the 27th inst. the battalion was relieved by the 8th Royal Irish Fusiliers, and moved back to brigade reserve in the hutments known as Kemmel Shelters. The camp was on the " safe " side of Mont Kemmel, and about two miles west of that village on the main Kemmel-Locre Road. Though the position was quiet from the shell point of view, it was most uninteresting and dull. Locre, a distance of about two miles and a-half from the camp, was the only centre of attraction in the district, and it was not advisable for the C.O. to allow the men away during the evening. As a matter of fact, the night time was our busy period for work. We supplied large fatigue parties each evening for work in the line.

After six days in support, we moved up again to the line and took over from the 8th Royal Irish Fusiliers in the same sector. One great advantage to this part of the line was the system of daylight reliefs. This was feasible partly because of the configuration of the ground, but more especially by the natural camouflage of the trees. The only precaution was to keep a good interval between companies in case of accidents. One never knew when the Boche might take it into his head to shell Kemmel village.

It was true the village had been knocked about from time to time by hostile artillery fire, but most of the damage was done near the batteries, or on chosen places such as " Suicide Corner " and the church. Both these latter spots were carefully avoided when moving up to relieve.

On taking over the line, " A " Company (Captain Morton) and " B " Company (Lieutenant A. E. C. Trimble) were disposed in the front line, " C " Company (Lieutenant Lilley) occupied S.P.'s nine and ten, and " D " Company (Lieutenant C. N. B. Walker) were in reserve at Regent Street dug-outs. The last-named position was a very favourite resort for the rat plague, and many campaigns of extermination were undertaken in quiet intervals. At no time, however, were the rats so plentiful as we had experienced them in the Loos Salient.

Captain D. H. Morton (O.C. " A " Company) was hit by a sniper in the head on the first day in the line, and Lieutenant H. W. Ruddock took over the company.

Rather an interesting coincidence at the time was the long stretch of front line held by service battalions of the Inniskillings— with the 36th (Ulster) Division on our immediate right, holding their left sub-sector with two battalions of Inniskillings, then ourselves, and again on our left the 8th Battalion.

On this trip we commenced putting into execution the scheme for the construction of proper shelters. With the assistance of the R.E. field company attached to the brigade, work was started on building a new company headquarters for the right company holding the front line system. The greatest difficulty the R.E. experts had to deal with was in the nature of the soil. It was impossible to dig down more than two feet deep without coming on water. As a result it was decided to erect a concrete shelter, above ground, heavily reinforced with steel girders. True, the dug-outs took a long time to complete, and when they were, it was extremely doubtful whether they were proof against anything of greater calibre than a field gun. The 8th Inniskillings and ourselves shared the work in the sector, handing over to each other on each successive relief.

On the 9th October we were relieved in the front system by the 8th Royal Irish Fusiliers, and then moved back into brigade support at Kemmel Shelters.

The C.O. (Lieutenant-Colonel K. C. Weldon), went on leave, and Major R. G. Kerr, recently appointed to field officer's rank, took over command in his absence.

In support, a certain amount of training was carried out by companies, but, as usual, the working parties rather interfered with this. Besides this, one company always remained forward in Kemmel Château in closer support. As a general rule, after the morning drill parades were finished, the men were free more or less for a few hours to do as they liked. This programme, of course, did not apply to the company in Kemmel, who, being under tactical notice to move at a moment's notice, devoted nearly all their time to improving and maintaining the defences in their own immediate vicinity.

Time passed quickly, if at times perhaps a little monotonous, and the 9th October saw us back again in the front system taking over the same sector from the 8th Royal Irish Fusiliers. The dispositions for the battalion were the same, with just a change round in the order of the companies. " C " Company (Lieutenant Lilley) and " D " Company (Lieutenant C. N. B. Walker) in the front line ; " A " Company (Lieutenant Ruddock) in S.P. eight and nine, " B " Company (Lieutenant A. E. C. Trimble) in reserve. Battalion headquarters, as usual, in Fort Victoria.

The medical officer (Captain G. O. F. Alley) found a corner in Regent Street dug-outs with the reserve company. For the M.O. and his staff the work was a change from the last six months. Our casualties were almost negligible, and up to this the men had suffered very little from trench fever and sickness. As the weather got worse later on, the number of sick increased, but was never serious at any time during the winter.

It must not be imagined that because our casualties were so slight that there was absolute peace on the front ; on the contrary, the sector was most dangerous at times. Activity had considerably increased since our first arrival in Kemmel, and it was now the common practice of the Boche to send over a considerable amount of heavy trench mortars at frequent intervals during the day. Most of these hostile efforts were directed on the top of Pall Mall, which was particularly annoying to us, as it was the only C.T. in our area. Piccadilly trench, on our right, was used occasionally as an emergency communication, but it was really within the next divisional area.

The constant damage to these linking trenches and *boyeaux* made the drainage problem more difficult. Although the weather was still favourable, it was easily apparent that unless some action was taken we should soon be flooded out. The reconstruction of Pall Mall was pushed forward as fast as the material was available, and the trench, when completed, had a waterway under the duckboards, about two and a half feet deep, which kept down the water satisfactorily, provided the trench was repaired immediately when blown in.

On the 21st October the battalion was relieved by the 8th Royal Inniskilling Fusiliers, and marched back to Locre and divisional reserve. In Locre the battalion was accommodated in a hutment camp just on the outskirts of the village in the

Rue de Bailleul. The officers' and various company messes were distributed throughout the houses in the village. This was the first occasion that we were billeted in Locre, and we did not make full use of the privilege. Later on we organised games, recreations and concerts, which made the period of divisional reserve very enjoyable. Very few fatigue parties were supplied by us, and the men appreciated their nights in bed.

Several " smokers " were held in the Y.M.C.A. and proved very successful. Many of our best performers had left the battalion at this time, but in spite of it, the programme was well up to our old standard. The regimental band played many selections, and Sergeant Joyce, Lieutenant Smythe, Private Phillips and others provided the individual talent.

On the 26th October we moved up the line again, and took over from the 8th Inniskillings. This time " A " and " B " Companies held the front system, with the other two companies in support. The C.O. (Lieutenant-Colonel K. C. Weldon) returned from leave the day after we moved into the front system, and the same day was appointed to command the recently amalgamated battalion, henceforth known as the 7/8th Royal Irish Fusiliers. The 2nd Royal Irish Regiment joined the 49th Infantry Brigade to make up the vacancy caused by the absorption of the R.I.F.

Major R. G. Kerr now assumed the temporary command of the battalion, with Lieutenant A. A. Seward as adjutant. Second-Lieutenant J. S. Foley was appointed assistant adjutant.

After the usual six days in the line, the battalion moved back to Locre, and for the whole month of November the reliefs worked out automatically, six days in the line and six days in Locre. Towards the end of the month the brigade carried out a " dummy raid " on the enemy's front line between Spanbroekmolen and Peckham. The 2nd R.I.R. and ourselves were holding the front system at the time. It was the first of these operations, and it was carried out with the intent of putting the " breeze up" the Hun, and at the same time inflict as many casualties on him as we could.

Zero hour was fixed for 6 p.m. on the 22nd November, and at zero, minus three minutes, a smoke cloud was discharged along the front. This action was followed at zero by an intense bombardment from the Divisional and Corps artillery. The T.M.B.'s co-operated in the general scheme, as did the machine-gun company. The barrage put down on the enemy's front line remained there for a space of two minutes, lifted to the support line for five minutes, and then switched back to the front line for another two minutes. No infantry action followed the bombardment, but the effort had the desired effect, as later in the evening our front line posts could distinctly hear the Boche bombing his own front line. It was astounding what a feeble reply the enemy's artillery gave to our barrage fire, though it must be admitted it was a consolation. Many minor operations of a like nature were undertaken by the division during the Winter of 1916, all with the same object of worrying the Hun. From the accounts of the Intelligence Staff it would appear that the schemes were most effective, and had the desired object of inflicting casualties on the Germans.

Another evidence of increased activity on the front was the order for the more frequent patrolling of " No Man's Land." The G.O.C. ordered that each man sent out on patrol at night must report in writing to his company commander the following morning what he had done during the night. These reports were sent to the Brigadier each day with the intelligence summaries for perusal. Some humorist, in writing an account of his adventures on patrol, wrote : " I was sent out last night with two other men and an N.C.O. as a listening patrol. It rained all night, and I got soaked to the skin in a shell hole. I saw nothing and I heard nothing ! "

On the 28th November, Major W. E. Rothwell, Royal Inniskilling Fusiliers, assumed command of the battalion during Major Kerr's absence on leave. He had only commanded the battalion for ten days when he was transferred to the command of the Second Army School of Musketry, and Major L. Farmer, 2nd Royal Irish Regiment, took over temporary command.

Behind the lines the 16th Division were getting comfortably fixed up for the winter, and much was done to amuse the men when out of the line. A divisional concert troupe was organised, and gave performances in the hall at Locre. So successful were the preliminary attempts that shortly afterwards the pierrot party got a pantomime going for the Christmas season. Many enjoyable evenings were spent at these entertainments during our frequent visits to Locre in reserve. The 36th (Ulster) Division on our right also started entertainments for their men, and on one occasion nearly a hundred other ranks of the battalion attended one of their concerts. " Q " Branch very kindly provided motor lorries for their transportation.

For the officers Bailleul was the great attraction, and with the assistance of the transport officer, who lent them horses occasionally, it became quite the " fashionable " resort whenever there was an opportunity of getting a day off.

On the 12th December the battalion moved into the front system, taking over from the 8th Inniskillings. During this period the weather became very bad indeed, and a lot of work had to be done to keep the trenches from collapsing in places. On our sector we were fairly lucky, as the communication trenches were all in good order after the recent work put in.

F

Regent Street—the main C.T. from Lindenhoek to the reserve line—was in most places little more than a naturally camouflaged track. Curiously enough, it was never made the target of the Boche artillery. At night when the enemy turned on his machine-guns, it became quite unpleasant, but we scarcely, if ever, had any casualties from this action. Presumably it was done in the hopes of catching ration parties going up the line, but men grew wise to this dodge, and used the road after dark. After the usual six days in the line, we moved back to Kemmel Shelters and brigade support. It was some time since we had occupied the support position, and nobody liked the change after the comparative luxury of Locre. It meant double the men for working parties, and nothing to do in our leisure hours. The sergeant's mess generally gave a concert to relieve the monotony. These entertainments were always well patronised by the officers, who, no doubt, still cherish happy memories of some of the evenings.

On the 23rd inst. another change in the command of the battalion took place. Major Farmer, 2nd Royal Irish Regiment, was posted to another unit, and Major R. G. Kerr became Commanding Officer.

The following day " The Seventh " went up to the front line. At the time we all cursed heartily that it should be our bad luck to be holding the front line on Christmas Day, but in many ways afterwards we were quite pleased. After all, it was an experience which might only come once in a lifetime, and as it turned out, it was quite peaceful. During the morning the Divisional Commander paid a visit to the battalion, and wished everyone the compliments of the season. The G.O.C. sympathised with our lot, but wished us the very best of luck in the New Year. Certainly, the General looked after his "boys" wherever they were, and had the knack of cheering up everyone with whom he came in contact. We learnt afterwards that he visited every unit in the Division on that day.

The C.O. went round all companies during the day, and exchanged greetings with the officers and other ranks. Practically, no hostile action took place all day—in fact, it was so quiet as to be uncanny. About dusk the Divisional Artillery fired a few salvoes over, but the enemy did not reply. The remainder of the evening was very quiet.

It was not for two days that either side began to liven up, and then the overture came from our side. At 2-15 p.m. on the 27th the enemy's defences along the whole brigade front were put through an intense bombardment from our guns for over an hour. " Heavies," Field Artillery, Medium Trench Mortars, Stoke's guns and Machine-guns all blazed away at their respective targets. Either the enemy was surprised, or still suffering from

the Christmas festivities, but he practically took no action.
The retaliation—what there was of it—was very feeble and
inaccurate.   We suffered no casualties as the result of the " strafe."

A few days more, and we were relieved on the 30th inst., and
went back to the " Shelters," where it was decided to make up for
the loss of Christmas by keeping the New Year, and giving the
men a really good feed.

On the 31st December the officers held a dinner in Kemmel
Château.   Incidentally, Major A. D. Reid and Captain V. H.
Parr, M.C., returned to the battalion during the afternoon, which
made the festival a particularly merry one to welcome them back.

From this date the battalion was taken over by Major A. D.
Reid, who was granted the acting-rank of Lieutenant-Colonel
whilst holding the position.

The first week of January, 1917, was spent by the battalion
in Kemmel Shelters, and very cold it was in huts which at the
best of times were not very comfortable.   New Year's dinner
and the New Year's Honours List did a lot to cheer people up.
Many of the honours included those who were recommended for
good work at the Battle of the Somme, and though they were
not all awarded on the 1st January, 1917, they are consolidated
for convenience in space.   A few of the decorations were awarded
at the end of October, 1916, and during November.

Distinguished Service Order—

Lieutenant-Colonel H. N. Young.

Military Cross—

Captain V. H. Parr.
Lieutenant G. A. C. Walker.
Major R. G. Kerr.

Military Medal—

18140 Corporal J. K. Frame.
27491 Private R. Semple.
21538 Private W. Richards.
23980 Private J. Boyle.
22981 Private W. Armstrong.
23113 Sergeant J. Smith.
25292 Private P. Flood.

Irish Brigade Parchment Certificate—
Captain V. H. Parr, M.C.
Lieutenant G. A. C. Walker, M.C.
25306 Private J. Russell.
27491 Private R. Semple, M.M.
27468 Private T. Dunn.

Mentioned in Despatches—
Lieutenant-Colonel H. N. Young, D.S.O.
Major A. D. Reid.
Lieutenant A. E. C. Trimble.

Up till the end of January, with the exception of a very successful raid on the 12th inst., there is little of importance to narrate. The usual trench sector was taken over by us periodically with a brief rest in Locre or Kemmel. The greatest discomfort suffered by the men was from the cold. Snow and frost were the order of the day for most of the month and, indeed, almost to the end of February.

The raid carried out on the 12th January was an excellent bit of work from every point of view. Under the command of Captain V. H. Parr, M.C. (who trained the raiding party for their task), Second-Lieutenant N. H. Woods and twenty other ranks went over to the Hun front line at 7-30 p.m. Within quite a short time they were safely back in our trenches, having captured two prisoners without suffering any casualties to the party. The Divisional Commander, in a letter to the C.O. on the following day, says : " I must send you a word of congratulation on " the good work done by the men of your battalion under Second- " Lieutenant Woods, last night, and on your own good arrange- " ments. They are just keeping up the record of the Seventh " Battalion."

As a result of the operation Second-Lieutenant Woods was awarded the Military Cross, and 28140 Private M. Sweeney (" B " Company) the Military Medal, for able assistance to the commander of the patrol.

The next event was the return to the battalion of Lieutenant-Colonel H. N. Young, D.S.O. On 15th February, 1917, almost the anniversary of leaving Bordon, he took over command. Captain A. C. Taggart, who rejoined the unit on the same day, took over the duties of adjutant. It is interesting to note that after a year's service in France " The Seventh " had done so creditably in its awards for gallantry in the field. No less than seventeen military medals, six military crosses, three " mentions," had been given to the battalion, not to speak of thirty-seven

Design made for Belt Plate (August, 1917).

"No Man's Land" near Vierstraat.

certificates of the Irish Division. The greatest honour of all was the battalion itself being mentioned in the Commander-in-Chief's despatch of May, 1916.

On the 27th February three new officers were posted to the battalion, and a small draft of men from the base depôt. Second-Lieutenants F. D. Morphy, H. P. H. Montgomery and T. J. D'Alton were the new arrivals. During the day the C.O. received instructions that the battalion were moving to Curragh Camp on the 2nd March; at the time " A " (Captain V. H. Parr, M.C.) and " B " Companies (Lieutenant A. E. C. Trimble) were in Derry Huts with " C " (Captain Seward) and " D " (Captain Stainforth) Companies in Kemmel Château.

The move to our new camp took place on the 3rd March, but not before the companies had the " satisfaction " of seeing Battalion Headquarters shelled with gas and lachrymatory shells. Naturally, the incident caused some anxiety to those who were subjected to the bombardment. It was quite a coincidence that a test gas-alarm had been arranged on this particular day, but the practical demonstration was quite sufficient for the purpose. One officer is reputed to have " opened a book " on the result of the strafe, and fortunately the betting went in his favour. Three hens and the destruction of the R.S.M.'s hut was the total damage.

Curragh Camp, on the Westoutre-Locre Road, was quite a pleasant situation, and never bothered by enemy shell fire. This was always a consolation in back billets, as somehow nobody ever expected to be shelled when behind the lines, and generally when they were, there was little or no cover to take if the shooting was at all accurate, which it often was. An officer's cross-country run was the cause of much amusement on the first day in camp. To their credit, nearly all of them finished the course, with the exception of two or three, who fell out in a state of exhaustion.

On 6th March the brigade held the boxing competition finals in the cinema hall at Locre. These events were warmly supported by all ranks, and the battalion was represented by Private W. Donoghue, " C " Company, in the welter weights. Donoghue, who was quite an exponent of the art before the war, won this event with ease.

Recreations and athletics were never organised so thoroughly and efficiently as they were during this period. Football matches were played off daily between the different companies, and the greatest enthusiasm was shown throughout the brigade to excel in the championships which were shortly to come. To add to these outdoor amusements for the men, the C.O. organised a pierrot troupe, which was known as the " Green and Buffs." This concert party, with the assistance of Captain Robinson

and Captain Seward, proved to be a great success. A star performance was given on the 13th inst. in Locre, which the Divisional
Commander, the Brigadier and Brigadier-General Ricardo (36th
Division) attended by invitation. These officers dined with
the C.O. and officers after the performance.

On St. Patrick's Day the C.O. gave the battalion a holiday,
and an inter-company cross-country run was held in the afternoon. After a very good race, " B " Company won. The first
three home were :—

    (1) Private M. Sweeney, M.M., " B " Company.
    (2) Private J. Herbert, " A " Company.
    (3) Sergeant T. Cunningham, Headquarters Company.

The evening was celebrated by companies in holding smoking
concerts, and judging by results they were a great success.

In Battalion Routine Orders, the same evening, was published
a list of officers and other ranks who were awarded " Irish Brigade
parchment certificates for gallant conduct in the field during
1916." The recipients were :—

    2/Lieutenant C. N. B. Walker.
    2/Lieutenant H. P. McKenna.
    13445 A/C.S.M. G. Dunn.
    28665 Corporal J. Glackin.
    26459 Corporal J. Maynes.
    3306 L/Corporal J. McCarthy.
    26501 Private N. Barry.
    22777 Private P. Kelly.
    3230 Sergeant A. Conway.
    9050 Sergeant W. Walden.
    26450 L/Corporal W. Fairless.
    27576 L/Corporal J. Brown.
    27068 Private W. Connolly.
    23280 Private G. Maguire.
    43200 Sergeant J. McCormick.
    7560 Sergeant R. Gillanders.
    24027 L/Corporal M. Firey.
    28686 L/Corporal J. McHale.
    28412 Private M. Sweeney.
    24635 Private T. Rice.

The next change of position for the battalion came on the 20th,
when we moved into brigade reserve at Butterfly Farm. The
relief was carried out in the forenoon. For four days the battalion
remained in this position, daily supplying fatigue parties for
work on the front line. Most of the work done was a continuation
of what we had been employed on whilst in the Curragh Camp, viz.,
extensive wiring operations in the second line. On the G.H.Q.
line further back we had erected acres of wire for its defence.

The idea of this policy was never quite clear, unless it was done as a bluff to the enemy to make it appear that we were on the defensive—in point of fact, we were on the eve of our preparation for the attack on the Wytschaete Ridge.

On 23rd March the battalion took over the front system from the 8th Inniskillings, with the following dispositions :—

Headquarters—York House.

" A " Company (Captain V. H. Parr, M.C.)—Lark Lane to Crowbar Trench (right).

" B " Company (Major R. G. Kerr, M.C.)—Crowbar Trench to Vierstraat Road (left).

" C " Company (Captain A. F. C. Graves)—S.P. 13 and Van Keep.

" D " Company (Captain C. H. Stainforth)—Watling Street.

For six days the battalion remained in the line, and then moved into brigade support, after a very quiet tour in the line. Nothing out of the ordinary took place until the end of the month, when we moved back to Clare Camp (Locre). It was the last time we held the line until after our preparation in the back areas for the great offensive.

. . . .

The Winter of 1916-17, though monotonous in that we held the same portion of line practically all through, was not quite so tedious as one would imagine. Although the wet and cold were factors in themselves, which caused us much unpleasantness at times, yet the distance to our billets and the nature of our work was not as wearisome as we had experienced the previous year in the Loos Salient. Undoubtedly, the amusements organised by the Divisional and Brigade staffs for the men went a long way towards making life more amenable. To add to this, we had profited by our experiences, and there were very few who hadn't a way of making things comfortable for themselves, even under the worst conditions. With very few exceptions, the N.C.O.'s and men who had come out with the battalion had been granted leave to the United Kingdom, and after all, one couldn't look further than that to keep up the *morale* of the troops.

CHAPTER VII.

THE BATTLE OF THE MESSINES-WYTSCHAETE RIDGE, 1917.

On the 13th April, 1917, the battalion, less " B " and " C "
Companies, left Birr Barracks (Locre) to march to the back areas
for training.   In reality, this move was the commencement of
our training for the never-to-be-forgotten Battle of Wytschaete.

At 8-35 a.m. the head of the column passed through the village
of Locre making south-west, along the main road to Bailleul.
The weather was ideal for the march, and everyone was in good
spirits at the thought of leaving the shelled area for a short spell.
It was not long before we reached Bailleul, and passing straight
through the "Grande Place" we swung to the right on to the
main Cassel road, the great highway to 2nd Army Headquarters,
and incidentally one of the best known supply traffic routes in
northern France.   Keeping to the main road until we reached
Meteren, we turned off to the left, and about a mile down the road
halted at the little village of Moolenacher.   Here we had a short
rest for dinner, and after the space of an hour we fell in about
1-30 p.m. and continued on towards Hazebrouck via Strazeele,
Pradelles and Borre.

By 3 p.m. we crossed the railway near the station at Hazebrouck,
and within fifteen minutes arrived at our destination for the night—
La Hte Loge.   The accommodation in billets was nothing wonderful, but there were no complaints.   After all, it was only for one

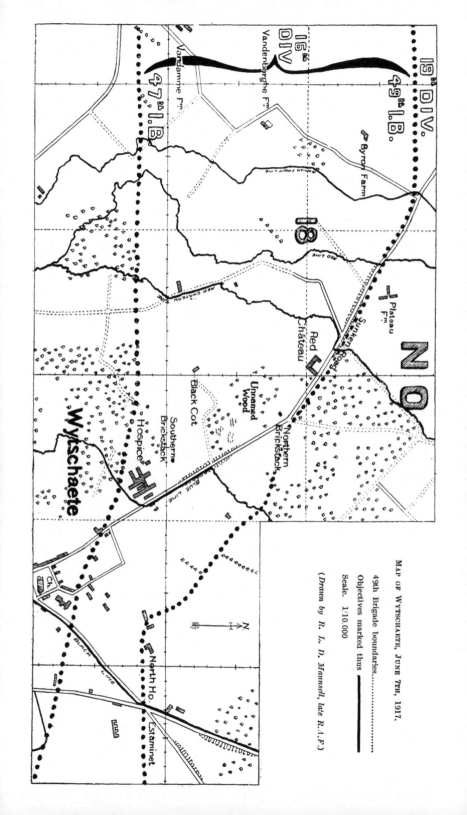

MAP OF WYTSCHAETE, JUNE 7TH, 1917.

49th Brigade boundaries.

Objectives marked thus ————

Scale. 1/10,000

(*Drawn by R. L. D. Mannell, late R.A.F.*)

night and, at any rate, we got somewhere to sleep, which was the main consideration.

The following morning the battalion started off about 8-15 o'clock. Though the distance to be covered was a few miles more than the previous day, the going seemed easier. This was due to the fact that the roads were not so crowded with motor transport as they had been nearer the line.

Our route lay through Ebblinghem—Renescure—Arques, and thence to Wizernes, where we stopped for the second night. The day's march was about sixteen miles, and nobody was sorry when we reached Wizernes. The heat of day, combined with the weight of equipment, made the journey very tedious. Be it said to their credit, not a man fell out on the march.

The 15th April was the last day of the trek. Unfortunately, it was not quite so pleasant as the two previous days had been. Rain fell during the morning and continued most of the day. Our destination was Zouafques, and by 3-45 p.m. the battalion arrived in billets. The road selected for the march was via St. Martin-au-Laert—Tilques—Moulle—Nordausques.

On arrival at billets we found " B " and " C " Companies waiting for us—they had come by motor transport during the day from Locre.

In such a delightful village as Zouafques we soon forgot the trenches and the shells, and settled down with renewed energy to commence training for our share in the great offensive. It was the first time, with the exception of a few days after we left the Somme area, that we had been out of the range of enemy shell fire for the last year. Needless to say, the change was welcome.

A general programme of training for the brigade was drawn up by the G.O.C., but on the whole, the C.O. exercised his powers in this respect as he wished. An adequate proportion of time was allotted to platoon, company and battalion training. The brigade field day was fixed for the end of the period, and was made the grand *finale* to our instruction.

The training area, east of Tournehem and about two miles south of Zouafques, was allotted to the brigade to carry out the above programme. The battalion left billets every morning and marched to the area for instruction, returning to Zouafques for dinner about 1 p.m. It was decided by the C.O., with the approval and consent of the Brigadier, that the afternoons should be devoted to games and recreations. The result of this scheme was the arrangement of many football fixtures between the different units in the brigade. A brigade championship was inaugurated in " Soccer " and " Rugger," which added greatly to the keenness of the men, and medals were presented to the winning teams in each event.

On the 19th April, the battalion was allotted the use of Range " B," 2nd Army Musketry School, near Moulle. The butts were about six miles east of Zouafques which meant setting out early to get the whole day on the range. On this occasion the field kitchens and Lewis gun limbers accompanied the battalion.

On arrival at the ranges, companies were detailed by the C.O. to various firing points, and practices were carried out independently by company commanders until dinner time. After dinner the C.O. decided on having some practice shooting from the Lewis guns. The result of this was a *battue* from every gun in the battalion (16). The Colonel was delighted with the " effective barrage " put down on the targets, and he ordered that all officers should fire the guns. The efforts of some of the officers to " get on " their targets were amusing, and the expenditure of S.A.A. hardly warranted the experience ! It was one of those training days enjoyed by everyone.

About 4 p.m. the battalion marched back to billets, and the following day being Sunday the troops were allowed to rest.

On the 21st April the preliminary rounds of the brigade championship were played off. At Association " The Seventh " beat Brigade Headquarters by 10 goals to nil, and at Rugby beat the 2nd Royal Irish Regiment by 9 points to nil. Both games created widespread interest throughout the brigade, and attracted an enthusiastic crowd of followers.

The 23rd saw us once again out for the day on the musketry ranges at Moulle. The programme was very similar to that carried out previously. Another demonstration was given on the effect of Lewis gun fire, but the most exciting episode of the day was the " advance " up to the butts in extended formation, firing from the hip. Several officers and others made remarks to the effect that it was better to be shot by the enemy than by odd rounds fired indiscriminately over the countryside ; however, no casualties were sustained as a result of the exercise.

The following day the brigade assault-at-arms was held on the training area at Tournehem. The competitions included Bomb-throwing, Retreat beating, Platoon drill and a Cross-country run. In the military items we were unlucky in that we only got second place in most of the events, but to compensate for this, 23618 Corporal Smith, " B " Company, secured first place in the run. In the bomb-throwing competition we were just beaten half a point by the 2nd Royal Irish Regiment after a keen contest.

The 26th April marked a most historic event in the history of the battalion : it was the great rehearsal brigade attack, carried out over the training area on replica trenches of the Wytschaete front; it was the finishing touch of preparation for the 49th Brigade.

The dispositions of the attack, even to the distance of the objectives, were identical with the subsequent arrangements, which are recorded in detail later in the final operation orders. The advance was carried out in the most realistic manner possible, and no amount of detail was spared to assist in its success. In front of the first wave was the " creeping barrage," cleverly substituted by a line of flag-waggers and side-drummers. These men moved according to the artillery schedule which was co-ordinated in the general idea. An unfortunate incident was occasioned by the fact that our men did not wear steel helmets as laid down in the routine orders of the day. Quite naturally, the Brigadier was displeased at our head-dress and demanded an explanation from the C.O. as to the reason for this " fooling." The C.O. said he thought the weather was too hot for steel helmets. The incident was soon forgotten in the excitement of the " attack."

The exercise was greatly stimulated by the presence of so many of the staff. Before the first objective had been captured, the whole area was seething with red tabs and inspecting general officers. The Brigade Commander, the Divisional Commander, the G.O.C. 9th Corps, and, greatest of all, the 2nd Army Commander (General Sir Herbert Plumer) were present. It made one almost tremble to see so much red and gold on the field, though it must be admitted it added a " dash of colour " to the proceedings.

At the conclusion of the operations the troops were allowed to fall out, and the officers were rallied to a conference to hear the various opinions of the scheme.

The Army Commander opened the debate by asking the various general officers for their views and tactical dispositions. The G.O.C. 49th Infantry Brigade opened the pow-wow with his opinion, and Major-General Sir W. B. Hickie and Lieutenant-General Hamilton Gordon followed with their ideas. It was, naturally, most interesting to hear what they had to say, but it was disappointing to note how much they criticised the efforts of the individual platoon commander. When the Corps Commander had finished speaking, General Sir Herbert Plumer gave a short lecture, in the course of which he amused the junior officers very much. He said that he never " strafed " anyone under the rank of a general officer !

In several instances he disagreed with the disposition of the Lewis guns and some other tactical details, but, on the whole, he was satisfied with the principles of the attack. He gave a most interesting discourse on the salient features of the plan of the real attack that was to come, and expressed a wish that the officers would explain to their men the objects for which they were fighting —it was the commencement of that great effort to clear the enemy, once and for all, out of Belgium and restore it back to its own people. At that time it was thought to be the beginning of the end.

The parade was dismissed after the conference, and the battalion marched back to Zouafques. In the afternoon, after a most exciting match, " The Seventh " beat the 8th Inniskillings by 2 goals to 1 in the semi-final of the Brigade Soccer Championship. The final was played the following day, but we were beaten, after a good game, by the 2nd Royal Irish Regiment.

Another practice attack took place on the 27th April, but this time it only concerned the battalion. Incidentally this was the anniversary of the enemy gas attack at Hulluch, just a year ago, and the following letter was received by the C.O. from the G.O.C. of the 16th (Irish) Division :—

" Will you please convey to all officers and men of the battalion
" under your command my good wishes to them on this the first
" anniversary of the defeat of the Bavarian attack at Hulluch.
" On that occasion the 7th Battalion nobly kept up the traditions
" of the Royal Inniskilling Fusiliers. I take this opportunity
" of expressing to all ranks my appreciation of the present spirit
" and smartness of the battalion."

The above was republished by the C.O. in battalion routine orders, and to this he added a paragraph in which he said : " I
" am absolutely confident that one and all intend to maintain the
" honour of your battalion and the glorious traditions of your
" regiment as you did so nobly a year ago.
" You have shown this spirit on every subsequent opportunity,
" and you will, I know, continue to do so in the future."

On the 28th April, the battalion left Zouafques for the Locre area. The journey back to the line was carried out with the identical arrangements that were made when we came down on the 13th May. The night of the 28th was spent in Wizernes, and the 29th in La Hte Loge.

The 30th was the last day of the trek, and on the way through Bailleul the Corps Commander (Lieutenant-General Hamilton Gordon) inspected the battalion on the march. The G.O.C. and his staff stood in the main square under the clock tower and took the salute. At the critical moment, as the head of the column drew near the saluting point, the adjutant's horse slipped on the *pavé* and came down. Fortunately, he managed to get the horse to his feet without any serious results, and the incident caused very little delay to the column.

About 4-45 p.m. the battalion reached Locre, where we fell out for dinner, and after a halt of two hours proceeded to the huts ments at Carnarvon Camp (about two miles north of Locre and a mile north-west of Westoutre).

During the six days' march, April 13th, 14th, 15th, 28th, 29th and 30th, the battalion covered just on 100 miles. Only one man fell out, and he had permission from the medical officer.

The approximate strength of the battalion when it arrived in camp was 30 officers and 670 other ranks, 55 horses, and the usual transport.

On the evening of the 30th April we received instructions that the 49th Infantry Brigade were taking over the Diependaal Sector on the night of the 1st-2nd May, and that we should move on the following day to Murrumbridgee Camp in brigade reserve.

In accordance with these orders we left camp the following morning and marched via La Clytte to our new billets. We remained here for the next five days. On the morning of the 4th May a draft of 18 men arrived from the base as reinforcements. Similar small drafts had joined on various dates during the last fortnight, which all assisted in bringing us up to full strength again.

On the night of the 5th-6th May came our turn to move into the front line in the Diependaal Sector. We relieved the 8th Inniskillings in the right sub-sector, and the boundaries taken over by the battalion were from Chicory Lane on the north to the Vierstraat-Wytschaete road (inclusive) on the south.

The dispositions adopted were :—

" C " Company (Captain Seward)—Right front line.

" D " Company (Captain C. H. Stainforth)—New Reserve trench, with one platoon under Second-Lieutenant J. Cunningham on the left of the front line.

" B " Company (Lieutenant A. E. C. Trimble)—Centre New Reserve.

" A " Company (Lieutenant W. T. Smythe)—New Reserve trench (right), with two platoons in Poppy Lane.

Battalion Headquarters were in dug-out shelters about half a mile north-west of Vierstraat.

The trenches in this sector, in so far as the front line was concerned, were practically only breastworks. The same difficulty was apparent in this sector as in all the trenches on the Flanders front. It was impossible to dig down any depth owing to the wet state of the country.

This tour in the line is memorable for the intense artillery bombardment by the enemy on the evening of the 9th May. As luck would have it, it was our last day in the line—in fact, the relief was just arriving in the trenches when the Boche put down a concentrated barrage on the New Reserve line. The enemy shooting was fairly accurate, though nothing exceptional. Undoubtedly, " D " Company on the left of the New Reserve line had the worst of it. Quite early in the bombardment " D " Company's headquarters and telephone dug-out were blown to pieces by

direct hits from 5.9's.   It seemed extremely likely at the time that
the enemy would raid under cover of this artillery fire, but,
curiously enough, the front line was only shelled intermittently
with high-bursting shrapnel.   On the right the shelling was not
quite so intense, and at no time was there any semblance of an
impending attack.   According to the reports from the O.C.
" C " Company, it would appear that the enemy had evacuated
his front and support lines.   Further evidence of this was shown
by the fact that after the bombardment had ceased the Huns
were heard bombing their way back to their own front line.   This
indicated " wind-up " rather than a contemplated offensive.

Matters on the left were becoming more and more serious as
time went on.   Captain W. H. Collis (only just rejoined the battalion) was killed by a direct hit of a 5.9.   Three other ranks were
killed, and 10 were wounded in " D " Company's line.   " B "
Company escaped with only one man wounded.

(Those who were killed in action during this bombardment
were buried in the new battalion cemetery at La Laiterie.)

By 10 p.m. the enemy had ceased firing, though our artillery
continued to fire for some time in retaliation.   There was no rifle
fire throughout the action.   Our Lewis guns, and the machine-
gunners covering us, opened fire on the enemy's front line when
the shelling commenced as a precaution against attack.

The relief was carried out when the situation was normal, and
the 7th Battalion East Lancs. Regiment (56th Infantry Brigade),
took over the sector.

The names of Captain C. H. Stainforth, Private Chisholme and
Private Dunn (all of " D " Company) were subsequently brought
to the notice of the G.O.C. for their coolness and gallant conduct
throughout the bombardment.

On completion of the relief, the battalion moved to De Zon
Camp, arriving in camp about 2 o'clock the following morning.
Here the battalion remained until the 14th inst., when it moved
up to the right sub-sector of the Vierstraat Sector, to take over
the line from the 2nd Royal Irish Regiment.

This tour in the line only occupied three days, and during that
time the situation on the front was normal.   One incident worth
mentioning was the trench mortar bombardment, assisted by
6-inch and 8-inch howitzers, which commenced at 3-15 p.m. on
the 15th inst.   The area selected for the shoot in the enemy's
lines was Petit Bois, and judging from ground observation, our fire
was very effective.   The enemy's retaliation to our fire was feeble.

On the 17th May we were relieved in this sector by the 8th
Royal Dublin Fusiliers, and on completion proceeded to Birr
Barracks (Locre), where we remained in Divisional Reserve until
June 3rd.

During this period the battalion supplied many fatigue parties for work in the forward zone.

Captain D. H. Morton rejoined the battalion, and assumed command of " B " Company. Second-Lieutenants W. G. Baker and A. H. Armstrong were posted to the battalion, and numerous drafts of men arrived, amounting in all to nearly 60 Other Ranks.

The ensuing fortnight at Birr Barracks was spent in preparation for the forthcoming offensive. The activity along the whole of the 2nd Army front was enormous. Every day saw fresh arrivals of field artillery and heavy guns. Dumps of ammunition, observation balloon sections, new aerodromes, etc., sprang up all over the country with astounding rapidity. From St. Eloi to Armentiéres the countryside was undergoing a metamorphosis—the essential arrangements were being completed before " zero day."

The work of the infantry on these occasions was mainly directed to strengthening and constructing shell-proof dug-outs that could withstand the inevitable preliminary artillery duel ; on digging trenches for the main telephone cable system ; on replenishing the stock of ammunition, bombs, rifle grenades, rockets and other material in the front line ; on planning and arranging the " assembly positions " to be used prior to the attack, and on detailing platoons and sections to the various duties allotted to them.

Before embarking on an attack on a large scale, all ranks must know the general idea of the scheme, otherwise they cannot co-operate successfully with the other troops. One Division, Brigade, or Battalion failing to achieve its particular object may lead to chaos and possible disaster along the whole front. This general idea was well represented by a model (made to scale), designed in clay, of the whole front to be attacked, which was carefully studied by our officers, N.C.O's. and men. The model was situated near Scherpenberg Hill.

For the Commanding Officer and his staff of specialists it meant the careful collaboration of the instructions regarding the front to be occupied by the battalion. Of course, the C.O. was nominally responsible for everything and anything that happened to his battalion, but at a time like this his work was chiefly directed to the compilation of operation orders and the study of the enemy's dispositions and trenches, from observation, aerial photography, and intelligence reports. Above all, the successful *liaison* with the other units co-operating and the administration for the welfare of his troops were important factors in the final issue. All these considerations meant constant work and thought, and no eventuality could be passed over in discussing the plans. Colonel Young never spared himself or his officers until he was satisfied that the arrangements were satisfactory, and even then minor details needed adjusting and checking right up to the last moment.

By the 30th May the instructions for the offensive were issued, together with the addenda and appendices relating to communications, artillery barrages and transport arrangements.

It would be quite impossible to recapitulate the operation orders *verbatim* owing to lack of space, but the general outline and plan of the main attack will be sufficient for the reader to grasp the action taken by the 2nd Army, more particularly as they concerned the 16th (Irish) Division and ourselves in consequence. The battalion arrangements are described more carefully, and the various main objectives and boundaries referred to are illustrated on Map facing page **88.**

The 2nd Army were attacking on a frontage held by three Army Corps, the main object of which was to capture and consolidate the ridge running almost north and south from Hill 60— Damnstrasse—Wytschaete—Messines—Ploegsteert.

On the success of the whole operation depended the ultimate attack on the Passchendaele Ridge in the autumn. It was hoped by the supreme command to co-operate with the naval forces on the Belgian coast, and in so doing to roll up the enemy's right flank and drive him out of Flanders before the winter. The realisation of these hopes and the partial success of the plans are by now well known to all. The attack to be carried out by the 9th Corps (the centre corps of the army) included the familiar names of Grand Bois, Petit Bois, Spanbroekmolen, Oostaverne Wood, and the village of Wytschaete, and the following divisions were detailed to carry out the opening phase of the offensive— the 19th Division (L), the 16th (Irish) Division (C), and the 36th (Ulster) Division (R).

On the front to be held by the 16th Division it was decided to attack with two infantry brigades in the line and one brigade in reserve, and accordingly the G.O.C. made his order of battle as follows :—On the left, the 49th I.B. ; on the right, the 47th I.B., with the 48th I.B. as Divisional Reserve.

Such being a *précis* of the general idea, we now turn to the action taken by the 49th I.B., and the part allotted to us in the Great Push.

The 49th Brigade were to advance on a two-battalion frontage, supported by the troops on either flank, and capture the four objectives, for convenience referred to as the " Red " line, the " Blue " line, the " Green " line, and the " Black " line. The units selected by the Brigadier and the general dispositions of the battalions in the Brigade were as follows :—The 7th Royal Inniskilling Fusiliers on the left front, and the 7/8th Royal Irish Fusiliers on the right front. To these two battalions were assigned the capture of the " Red " and " Blue " lines. The 2nd Royal Irish Regiment on the capture of the first two objectives were ordered to move

VILLAGE OF WYTSCHAETE AFTER THE ATTACK. (*Block lent by H.M. Stationery Office.*)

forward and take the " Green " and " Black " lines respectively. The 8th Royal Inniskilling Fusiliers were detailed to act as " moppers up " to the brigade.

On the 2nd June, 1917, the battalion left Birr Barracks (Locre), and moved forward to Butterfly Farm, taking over from the 7th Royal Irish Rifles. Before leaving Locre the C.O. detailed the officers and other ranks who were to remain out of the line for the " show." The *personnel* left behind were referred to as " B " echelon, and the senior officer acted as O.C. Rear Headquarters.

Whilst in Butterfly Farm the men's equipment was inspected frequently to make certain that their gas respirators, rifles, etc., were kept in a serviceable condition and ready for immediate use. Companies and platoons were lectured on their duties, and stores were issued in anticipation of the approach of zero day. At this time it was unknown to us what the date and hour of zero would be, but it was obvious from the advanced state of the preparations that it was not far distant.

The guns along the whole corps front were in position almost wheel to wheel, and were busy registering all day. The heavies fired many rounds during this time on hostile batteries and on selected targets for demolition. The enemy retaliation to our methods was chiefly concentrated on the battery zone, with spasmodic bursts of harassing fire on the trench lines. A large quantity of gas shells were employed by the Boche, and for the first time we came under fire from mustard gas shells. Our gas respirators were proof against all forms of gas, and this gave us great confidence. The important point was to be always on the alert and don our helmets in time. On some occasions casualties were caused by delay in putting on the helmets after the bombardment commenced ; this was inevitable.

A clever ruse for ascertaining where the Boche fire would come when we attacked and also for spotting how much artillery the enemy actually had opposite us was resorted to in the idea of the practice barrage. This practice barrage was fired from our guns according to the identical programme laid down for the real attack. To those who had an opportunity of watching the spectacle from Kemmel Hill it was a wonderful sight. Cunning as the idea was, the Hun was not " drawn " by the operation. The retaliation was not up to expectations. In many ways this was a relief to our minds, as we sincerely hoped that the enemy would take the same action when we eventually did go over the top. In point of fact, the German guns never did take any very serious action until some considerable time after zero. It is understood that most of the enemy fire was directed on Yprés and on the southern flank towards Ploegsteert and Armentiéres.

G

It was unlucky that R.S.M. Dolan should have been hit on the 4th inst.   This was the second occasion in the last eight months.

On 5th June the C.O. was notified by secret letter that zero day would be on the 7th inst.   The exact hour was not published until later.   By the same D.R. came the following letter from the 16th (Irish) Division Headquarters at Westoutre :—

" The Big Day is very near.   All our preparations are complete,
" and the Divisional Commander wishes to express his appreciation
" and his thanks to all the officers and men who have worked so
" cheerfully and so well.   The 16th Division is fortunate in having
" had assigned to it the capture of the stronghold of Wytschaete.
" Every officer and man—gunners, sappers, pioneers, R.A.M.C.,
" A.S.C., and infantrymen of historic Irish regiments—knows
" what he has to do.

" Let all do their best, as they have always done, continuing
" to show the same courage and devotion to duty which has
" characterised the 16th (Irish) Division since it landed in France,
" and it will be our proud privilege to restore to Little Belgium,
" the ' White Village,' which has been in German hands for nearly
" three years.

" (Signed) W. B. HICKIE,

" *Major-General,*

" Commanding 16th (Irish) Division.

" 5th June, 1917."

Both of the above orders were communicated to the company commanders by the Colonel at a final conference held at Butterfly Farm.   This conference, like many similar functions of its kind, held from time to time, was convened at short notice, and on this occasion rather an amusing incident occurred.   The adjutant despatched orderlies to the company commanders with a verbal message that they were required at Battalion Headquarters *at once*.   In due course the commanders of " A," " B " and " C " Companies arrived at the " Holy of Holies," saluted the C.O., and waited their orders.   The C.O. looked up from the table, and said : " Has anyone seen Captain Stainforth ? "   No reply was forthcoming.   Another orderly was sent to " D " Company, and returned in a few minutes with a message from Captain Stainforth that he was dressing but would be along directly.   Yet another orderly was despatched with a message that he must come at once and as he was !   Five minutes after the final summons, the O.C. " D " Company appeared in his shirt sleeves, with half one side of his face shaved, and a wobbling brush in his right hand. His general turn-out was so *bizarre* that even the C.O. almost smiled at him, but nothing happened. Business was carried on as usual, and incidentally lasted nearly an hour and a half ; the " soap " by then had become like crystallised sugar. The punish ment had been made to fit the crime !

In the evening the battalion took over from the 8th Royal Inniskilling Fusiliers in the left sub-sector of the Vierstraat Sector. The dispositions were as follows :—

> " B " Company (Lieutenant Trimble)—(Front line) from N.18 a. 50.00 to the junction of Vierstraat road, with front line trench.

> " A " Company (Second-Lieutenant G. L. Henderson)— Reserve line (the Park and Chinese Wall line).

> " D " Company (Captain C. H. Stainforth) } Vierstraat Switch (immediately east of the Vierstraat- Kemmel road).
> " C " Company (Captain A. A. Seward)

Second-Lieutenant A. H. H. Armstrong took over the duties of assistant adjutant *vice* Second-Lieutenant C. H. Ffolliott, sent down to field ambulance sick.

No unusual activity took place in the line on the night of the relief ; in fact, considering all the circumstances, the line was abnormally quiet. A certain amount of gas shelling took place in the battery zone, but nothing of a very concentrated nature in our area.

It was always difficult in the front system to locate back shelling, but the following morning we ascertained that the enemy had been very busy on the batteries in a vain attempt to silence them.

On the night of the 6th-7th June the battalion commenced clos-ing up to its assembly positions. Strict orders were issued regarding lights, and no man was allowed to smoke or show any light in the front line. Before midnight the companies had taken up their allotted positions, and from that time remained silently awaiting the signal of " zero " at dawn. Rather a weird thing happened about 1 a.m. when a Boche aeroplane, flying very low, came over our front line. The pilot was evidently looking for signs of activity, but got little satisfaction for his trouble. The order of battle within the battalion was as follows :—

> " A " Company (Second-Lieutenant G. L. Henderson)— Front line from N.18a. 55.00 to a point 50 yards north of Mayo Street (communication trench from front to support line).

" B " Company (Lieutenant A. E. C. Trimble)—50 yards north of Mayo Street to the Vierstraat road (inclusive).

" C " Company (Captain A. A. Seward)
" D " Company (Captain C. H. Stainforth)

{ Shannon Trench from N.18a. 35.00. to the Vierstraat road (inclusive).

Battalion Headquarters was in Usnagh Street (N.18a. 15.415).

Companies and other units attached to the battalion for general co-operation in the attack were officially reported to be in position by 1-35 a.m.

The late arrival of the transport officer with the rations was the source of some well-founded anxiety at Battalion Headquarters. This was explained by the congested state of the roads with constant traffic throughout the night. Captain V. H. Parr, M.C., acting second-in-command for the time, supervised the issue of food to the companies in front, and Lieutenant Reid just managed to get his horses and wagons clear of the forward zone before the bombardment opened. Later in the day this officer took over the control of the brigade pack mules, and distributed supplies to the troops after the attack. The weather was so hot that the transport of water was a most essential requisite. Within three hours of the initial attack, the men in the outpost line were supplied with all their requirements. The work of the transport *personnel* and quartermaster's staff was most efficient

At 3-10 a.m. on 17th June, 1917, the battle commenced, and promptly at the appointed hour the mines went up under the enemy's front line at various points along the army front. The nearest explosions to us were the mines at ——————, and at Petit Bois. Neither of these were actually opposite our particular line. In a moment the sky was lit up and the ground shook like an earthquake for miles round. To those in the front line, it almost felt as though the parapet would fall in on top of them. The whole area seemed to sway with the vibrations. (We afterwards learnt that an aggregate of 937,000 lbs of explosive had been used along the front). For a time it was impossible to see more than ten yards across " No Man's Land," the air was so thick with smoke and dust.

Simultaneously with the fall of our barrage the companies advanced across the open. " A " Company on the right, and " B " Company on the left formed the first two waves. " C " and " D " Companies followed in the rear as the third and fourth waves. A distance of 100 yards interval was maintained between the waves.

PANORAMA OF THE WYTSCHAETE RIDGE.

(1) Zero Wood.   (2) Onraet Wood.   (3) Wytschaete.
(4) Grand Bois.   (5) Unnamed Wood.   (7) Wytschaete Wood.
(9) German Front Line.   (6) The Hospice.   (8) Petit Bois.

At first, no enemy action hindered the assault in any way. In the opening stages, the greatest impediment to our progress was caused by our own action. The dense clouds of smoke and dust caused by the explosions of the mines made it very difficult to see more than a few yards ahead in places. In many cases the men were obliged to don their gas respirators owing to the extreme difficulty of breathing in the thick atmosphere. The air on some parts of the front did not clear for nearly two hours after zero.

On reaching the enemy front line the barbed wire bore ample testimony of the efficiency of the damage done by our artillery. No delay was made in the outpost line, as it was practically evacuated by the Germans, and within a few moments the advancing waves pressed on to the support line. Strictly adhering, so far, to the operation orders we took the first battalion objective (Nail Switch) in twenty minutes. Here no trace of a line could be found, having been blotted out by our shell fire, and as the position was un-favourable—consisting of a swamp—the forward companies moved on towards the Red Château line.

Up to this there were very few casualties, and any there were had mostly been caused from our creeping barrage. This may seem a striking admission to the reader, nevertheless it is true. In all trench attacks at this stage of the war it was found by experience to be essential to keep the forward troops close on the heels of the barrage. Failing this, the result would probably mean annihilation from enemy machine guns. Of the two evils, the former was the most profitable and much more economical.

Within a short space of time the troops arrived at the Red Château line. " A " Company—who were at this time com-manded by Lieutenant H. W. Ruddock—met with some opposi-tion from small parties of the enemy who had reorganised them-selves and were established in shell holes to resist the attack. These remnants offered very little resistance, and were quickly dealt with. Some prisoners were taken by this company and sent back by the " Moppers Up."

On the left " B " Company (Lieutenant A. E. C. Trimble) captured some batches of the enemy hiding in dug-outs on the Sunken road (the Vierstraat-Wytschaete Road). Great delight was caused in finding German beer, cigarettes and soda water in many of the dug-outs. In some cases breakfast was ready, the Hun had fled, leaving everything, when the attack was launched. No serious opposition was met with on the left up to this point. Most of the captured Boches appeared to be dazed from the effects of our mines and barrage.

The Red Château line did not prove to be a satisfactory position to consolidate, and after a time the O.C. "A" Company decided to move his men forward. " B " Company were informed of the proposed move, and eventually both these companies consolidated on the " Red " line after " C " and " D " Companies had passed through.

The " Red " line (battalion third objective) was captured by " C " and " D " Companies. A halt was made after it was taken, before proceeding to the " Blue " line, and about 4-25 a.m. these companies continued their advance. Keeping close up to their protective fire, they stormed the ridge, capturing Unnamed Wood on the left and the Hospice and northern portion of the Bois de Wytschaete on the right. During this final manoeuvre of the battalion the enemy showed very little resistance. So completely demoralised was he from the initial success all along the line that in many parts the trench lines, such as they were, were deserted.

" D " Company (Captain C. H. Stainforth) experienced some machine-gun and rifle fire whilst passing through Unnamed Wood, but none of these actions hampered their advance. The " Blue " line was completely ours by 4-45 a.m., and the two forward companies soon got in touch and established communication with the units on either flank—the Welsh Regiment (19th Division) on the left, and the 7/8th Royal Irish Fusiliers on the right.

The next item on the artillery schedule was to " pile up " fire in front of our outpost line in order to prevent any counter-attack being organised before the objective had been consolidated. No counter-attack was attempted until much later in the day, and even then it was half-hearted and not pushed with any vigour. The field artillery disorganised the enemy's troops and communications so thoroughly that, for the time being, at any rate, it took the Huns some little time to restore their front.

During the time the attack had been progressing, the signal officer (Lieutenant H. P. Montgomery) was employed in linking up the various means of communications with the main brigade forward system. When telephone lines were satisfactorily established, the C.O. and his Battalion Headquarters' staff moved forward to the western edge of Unnamed Wood.

At 6-50 a.m. the 2nd Royal Irish Regiment passed through the " Blue " line and advanced to capture the final objectives of the 49th Infantry Brigade—the " Green " and " Black " lines. From this time forward our position as a battalion became one of close support to the attacking troops. Work was concentrated on digging strong points at selected places in the battle area, and on making the line secure in case of counter-attack.

Later in the day the 33rd Infantry Brigade went through the 2nd Royal Irish Regiment, and advanced to the " Mauve Line " east of Oostaverne Wood. By that time the enemy had a chance to recover his senses, after the first shock, and use his reserve units. The reserves, however, were not able to stop the advance, and the furthest objective was captured by 3-10 p.m.

It was a wonderful sight to see the field artillery coming into action in " No Man's Land." Galloping up from the rear of our old front line system they got over the trenches by the bridges which had been previously erected, and in a very short time were barraging the enemy's defences at Oostaverne.

At 8 a.m. our orders were that we should be relieved from our positions at dusk that evening, and move back to our old lines. This move took place without any mishap about 9 o'clock on the night of the 7th. As our troops were relieving, an S.O.S. signal was sent up from the front line calling for a protective screen of artillery fire owing to counter-attack. The counter-attack—if such it was—never materialised and the line remained intact.

Back in our old lines around the Chinese Wall (now almost reserve areas) we had an opportunity of checking and counting up the casualties. The first lists submitted were, naturally, not quite accurate, as it always happened in big operations that men were reported missing possibly because they had escaped the notice of an officer or a N.C.O. when hit.

The final casualty list was not compiled for nearly a fortnight. It is now republished for information, and a study of the table will be sufficient evidence of the lightness of our casualties in comparison to the objectives gained and the magnitude of the enterprise.

(A)	" A " COY.		" B " COY.		" C " COY.		" D " COY.		H'QRS		TOTALS	
	OFF.	O.R.	OFF.	O.R.	OFF.	O.R.	OFF.	O.R.	OFF.	O.R.	OFF.	O.R.
Strength on June 7th	4	125	4	124	5	118	4	119	5	73	22	559
Do. June 8th	1	94	3	84	4	76	2	74	5	73	15	401
(B) Killed in Action	—	3	—	3	—	5	—	2	Nil.		—	13
Died of Wounds	—	—	—	2	1	1	1	4	Nil.		*2	7
Wounded	3	27	1	36	—	36	1	39	Nil.		5	138
Wounded (at duty)	Nil.		Nil.		1	3	—	1	—	1	1	5
Missing	Nil.		Nil.		Nil.		Nil.		Nil.		Nil.	
TOTALS	3	30	1	41	2	45	2	46	—	1	8	163

*2/Lieut. H. E. Linde and 2/Lieut. T J. Dalton.

Rumour was current on the 8th that we were being withdrawn from the line to reorganise for a further attack. This was unfounded. As it turned out, we moved back to Wicklow lines in Locre on the evening of the 9th inst., and on arrival in billets we found the G.O.C. (Major-General W. B. Hickie) was waiting to congratulate the C.O. and the men on their success.

As the companies arrived in billets, the Major-General waved his hand to them, saying " Well done ' The Seventh,' the war is nearly over now."

The next day the whole division was taken out of the line, and the following letter was received from the Divisional Commander:—

" The 16th Division has been relieved to-day. For over eight " months we have held our portion of line, and we can look back " with pride and satisfaction to the record of those months. " Neither rain or snow, or the heat of summer has interfered with " the constant work.

" Long distances, wet roads, cold nights, shortage of fuel have " all failed to damp the spirits of the men.

" With gun and howitzer, trench mortar, rifle, machine-gun " and bomb, and sometimes with bayonet, we have gradually " worn down the boasting enemy ; and two days ago, with small " losses to the division, we have completed this chapter of our " history by taking from him the wood and village of Wytschaete, " and the crest of the hill, which means so much for future " operations.

" The Divisional Commander, in congratulating all ranks of the " division on their victory of June 7th, thanks all the officers, " N.C.O's. and men under his command for their loyalty and " help, and for their bravery and skill in action. Whatever new " work lies before us, it will be tackled with the same endurance, " the same cheerfulness, and the same bravery ; and again and " again the division, and every man in it, will justify the right " to our motto : ' Everywhere and always Faithful.' "

The Major-General was so pleased with the work of the battalion in the attack that he granted the C.O. permission to erect a notice board in Unnamed Wood with its new name inscribed on it— " INNISKILLING WOOD."

It is well known to all by now the effect and success of the battle of the Messines-Wytschaete Ridge, and it is therefore unnecessary to dwell on the strategical advantage gained by the enterprise. From our point of view, as a battalion, it was a " walk over." The weather was ideal, the casualties surprisingly light, and the staff organisation irreproachable. No detail was left unconsidered beforehand, with the result that when the signal came to take our objectives we advanced with confidence under a most powerful and efficient artillery support. To all intents and purposes it was a gunner victory almost entirely. The Hun was blown out of his positions, and so thoroughly demoralised was he by the efficacy of the bombardment that he threw up the sponge quite early in the proceedings. The enemy admits the extraordinary power of explosive used against them. General Ludendorff says :

" At the beginning of June increased activity on the part of " the enemy was noticeable in the neighbourhood of our salient " at Wytschaete, south of Ypres. The straightening of this " salient really ushered in the great Flanders battle in June. As " long as it remained in German hands every British attack at " Ypres and to the north of that town was outflanked from the " south . . . we should have succeeded in retaining the " position but for the exceptionally powerful mines used by the " British, which paved the way for their attack, consisting, as " usual, of fierce artillery fire supporting a closely massed infantry " advance. The result of these successful mining operations was " that the enemy broke through on June 7th. . . . The " 7th June cost us very dear, and owing to the success of the enemy " attack the drain on our reserves was very heavy. Here, too, " it was many days before the front was again secure."

Sir Douglas Haig published a special order on the following day (the 8th) which is interesting in contrast to the above account.

" SPECIAL ORDER OF THE DAY.

" The complete success of the attack made yesterday by the " 2nd Army, under the command of General Sir Herbert Plumer, " is an earnest of the eventual final victory of the Allied cause.

" The position assaulted was one of very great natural strength, " on the defences of which the enemy had laboured incessantly " for nearly three years. Its possession, overlooking the whole " of the Ypres Salient, was of the greatest tactical and strategical " value to the enemy.

" The excellent observation which he had from this position " added enormously to the difficulty of our preparations for the " attack, and ensured to him ample warning of our intentions. " He was therefore fully prepared for our assault and had brought " up reinforcements of men and guns to meet it.

" He had the further advantage of the experience gained by " him from many previous defeats in battles such as the Somme, " the Ancre, Arras, and Vimy Ridge. On the lessons to be drawn " from these he had issued carefully thought out instructions.

" Despite all these advantages the enemy has been completely " defeated. Within the space of a few hours all our objectives " were gained, with undoubtedly very severe loss to the Germans.

" Our own casualties, for a battle of such magnitude, were most
" gratifyingly light. The full effect of this victory cannot be
" estimated yet, but that it will be very g.eat is certain.

" Following on the great successes already gained it affords
" final and conclusive proof that neither strength of position nor
" knowledge of and timely preparation to meet impending assault
" can save the enemy from complete defeat, and that, brave and
" tenacious as the German troops are, it is only a question of how
" much longer they can endure the repetition of such blows.
" Yesterday's victory was due to causes which always have given
" and always will give success, viz.—the utmost skill, valour and
" determination in the execution of the attack following on the
" greatest forethought and thoroughness in preparation for it.

" I desire to place on record here my deep appreciation of the
" splendid work done above and below ground, as well as in the
" air, by all Arms, Services, and Departments, and by the Com-
" manders and Staffs by whom, under Sir Herbert Plumer's
" orders, all means at our disposal were combined, both in prepara-
" tion and in execution, with a skill, devotion and bravery beyond
" all praise.

" The great success gained has brought us a long step nearer to
" the final, victorious end of the war, and the Empire will be justly
" proud of the troops who have added such fresh lustre to its arms.

" (Signed) D. HAIG,

" *Field-Marshal,*

" Commanding-in-Chief,

" British Armies in France.

" Advanced G.H.Q.,
   " 8th June, 1917."

Many messages of congratulation were received during the
next few days from various unit commanders. The corps commander wiring to the 16th (Irish) Division, said :

" The Army Commander wishes me to convey to all ranks his
" warmest congratulations and his appreciation of the splendid
" work they have done on the 7th inst.

" Well done 16th Division. Heartiest congratulations on
" capture of Wytschaete. I fully realise what a magnificent
" effort by each individual has been."

Our stay in Locre was a brief one and was occupied most of the
time by supplying enormous fatigue parties up the line for work
on making up the roads and tracks which had been so damaged
by artillery fire in the battle area. In many ways these working

parties were interesting, as they gave us ample opportunity of studying the visibility from the ridge which the Germans had enjoyed for so many months. Great interest was taken by all ranks in examining the colossal craters made by our mine explosions. In many cases a couple of houses could have been nicely hidden in the cavities.

On the 13th June the battalion was released from duty as a unit, and started off at 7 a.m. to march to the Merris area (two miles south of Meteren) for a rest. On the following day the C.O. published in orders the names of those officers and men who had been rewarded for their services in the field by H.M. the King on the occasion of his birthday :—

Major A. D. Reid—Distinguished Service Order.
Captain G. O. F. Alley (M.O.)—Military Cross.
Captain A. C. Taggart (adjutant)—Mentioned in Despatches.
Captain A. A. Seward   do.
Captain the Rev. Father Kelly, C.F.   do.
15013 R.Q.M.S. Wilson, R.   do.
21109 Sergeant Stafford, S. (Transport) do.
21178 Private O'Donnell, J.   do.
24635 Private T. Rice—Croix de Guerre (France).

During our stay in Merris we received instructions to return to Locre on the 16th June. In accordance with these orders we set out on the 17th inst., marching via Meteren, Schaexken, and Croix de Poperinghe, and arrived in Clare Camp about 10 o'clock. The exact reason for this sudden move back to the line was never quite clear, but we got orders, almost immediately on arrival in Locre, to move off again the following day back to Merris. This we did, arriving back in billets at 8-45 o'clock on the morning of the 18th.

On the 19th June the Brigade Commander inspected the battalion in Merris, and gave an address to the men at the conclusion :

" Officers, N.C.O's. and men of the Fighting 7th Royal Innis-
" killing Fusiliers, a few days ago General Plumer came and asked
" me to congratulate you on his behalf, on the most excellent work
" which had been done by you on the morning of the 7th June.
" He pointed out the immense strategical and tactical value of
" the German position on Wytschaete Ridge, which had been
" wrested from them by the valour and determination of the
" British. He also said that this attack was considered to be
" quite one of the best attacks the British Army had ever made,
" and so you can all be proud that you have taken part in it.
" The Germans had no intention of losing that ridge, but owing
" to the good work of all ranks, they did. You must remember
" these big fights are historic, and this action will be held up to

" your sons as a battle well worth studying, and your sons will
" say, ' My father was there.'

"I must congratulate you also on your turn-out this morning ;
" you are a credit to the regiment you belong to.   If soldiers are
" not smart and proud of themselves they are of no use.   You
" are, and you have every reason to be so."

As a result of the operations on the 7th June, the following
decorations and honours were bestowed on members of the
battalion for conspicuous gallantry.

Military Cross—
Captain C. H. Stainforth.

Distinguished Conduct Medal—
26457 Corporal J. Maynes.

Military Medals—
20157 Private J. Crowe.
18409 Private C. Ward.
 3286 Private T. Norney.

Parchment Certificates—
Lieutenant H. W. Ruddock.
2/Lieutenant F. D. Morphy.
2/Lieutenant H. P. H. Montgomery.
13098 Sergeant T. Cunningham (A/R.S.M.).
18116 Sergeant T. J. Morris.
26487 Corporal T. J. Maynes,
26674 Corporal J. Taylor.
26420 L/Corporal W. Fairless.
30199 L/Corporal Sutherland.
24898 L/Corporal Rigby.
 3274 Sergeant Edgell.
 9178 Sergeant F. Heaney.
21109 Sergeant Stafford.
21230 Corporal G. McGarry.
20853 Private E. Chisholm.
20871 Private M. Smith.
25096 Private J. Deerey.
28140 Private M. Sweeney.
 2386 Private T. Norney.
26620 Private P. Quigley.
18409 Private C. Ward.
20175 Private J. Crowe.

MAP OF THE ATTACK ON AUGUST 16TH, 1917 (YPRES).

Scale 1/20,000

Brigade Boundaries . — . — . —
Objectives ————

(Drawn by R. L. D. Mauncell, late R.A.F.)

CHAPTER VIII.

THE THIRD BATTLE OF YPRES.

Eecke—Training at Buysscheure—Major A. D. Reid, D.S.O., leaves the battalion—Winizeele—The march from Watou to " B " Camp via Poperinghe—A bad night in bivouacs near Vlambertinghe—Relieved the 8th Inniskillings on 6th August—Our dispositions in the line—Activity on the night of the 7th—Back in reserve billets—Instructions and operation orders for the offensive—Moving up to the attack—Zero on 16th August—Progress of the assault—Beck House and Delva Farm captured—Captain Parr's report on the situation—Relieved on night 16th-17th—The amalgamation with the Eighth—Special orders by Lieutenant-Colonel H. N. Young, D.S.O.

The 20th June saw us once more on trek—this time quite a short march to the village of Eecke, about five miles N.W. of Caestre. In favourable weather, such as we had at that time, we thoroughly enjoyed moving about the back areas. The change from the routine life in the trenches was highly appreciated by all ranks. The day's work was generally finished by lunch time, and for the rest of the day the men were quite content to remain in billets and enjoy a good rest. After all, we never knew the date or the hour when we might be ordered back to the line again for duty. Rumours were already abroad that the " salient " had been taken over by the Fifth Army (General Sir H. de la Poer Gough) preparatory to the opening of the next offensive—the Battle of the Passchendaele Ridge.

Our stay in Eecke was a short one and not altogether exciting. After two days we packed our baggage and set out for Buysscheure, near St. Omer. This was a longer march than usual, and necessitated an early start being made. In more ways than one this was an advantage, as by doing this we avoided the intense heat n the middle of the day and also the increased lorry traffic on the roads. On this march the battalion had the honour of being inspected by the G.O.C. Second Army (General Sir Herbert Plumer, G.C.M.G., etc.). The Army Commander was mounted and took the salute as the men marched through Zuytpeene. By 10-30 a.m. the battalion arrived in its new billeting area, and the men were allowed to rest for the remainder of the day.

It was in the Buysscheure area that we commenced training again in real earnest.   Companies were given a free hand to carry out their own schemes, with an occasional field-day organised by the C.O., which generally took the form of an open attack across country.   The vicinity was ideal for field operations.

An inspection by the Divisional Commander on the 29th inst. terminated our programme at Buysscheure, and after an early start the next morning we set out for Zudausques.   Our route on this march lay through St. Momelin, St. Omer and St. Martin-au-Laert.   We reached Zudausques at 9-30 a.m.

From this on through the month of July, 1917, we spent a most peaceful existence behind the lines training and reorganising for the offensive at Ypres.   It was a period full of work and plenty of recreation that will ever retain pleasant memories of the good times we enjoyed together out of the line.   It was unique, but uneventful.

On the 5th we moved to camp at Tatinghem, and it was here that we bade farewell to one of the oldest and truest supporters of the battalion—Major A. D. Reid, D.S.O.   For close on three years he served with " The Seventh," during which time he worked indefatigably for the good of the battalion, and in return had won the respect of all with whom he came in contact.   Within a month of his departure he was killed whilst in command of the 1st Royal Irish Rifles.   Colonel Young, in writing to the " Sprig," said : " It was due to him, and he alone, that the magnificent spirit of " *esprit-de-corps* and bond of true brotherhood existed between " all ranks.   His loss was deeply felt by all who knew him and " had served under him."

By the 9th July we had moved to canvas in the Winizeele area. Here we remained for a few days over the fortnight, when the division was concentrated in reserve before the opening of the third battle of Ypres.   Nothing of interest remains to be said of our stay in Winizeele except that the weather treated us most favourably.   A welcome visitor to the officers' mess on the 24th inst. was our first commanding officer, Colonel R. C. C. Cox. Being stationed in the vicinity he paid us a call, and stayed to dinner afterwards with the C.O. and officers.

It was on the 30th July, after four days in camp near Watou, that we moved into the shell zone once again.   Marching through Poperinghe that evening we got some idea of the enormous scale of the new offensive.   As usual, the roads were *choc-à-bloc* with transport vehicles and motor lorries.   Everything seemed to be moving in one direction only—to the salient.   About midnight we were marching up the main Ypres-Poperinghe road, and

MAJOR ALEXANDER D. REID, D.S.O.,
Killed in Action—July 31st, 1917.

before 1-30 a.m. we reached " B " Camp (two miles S.W. of Vlambertinghe), where we fixed up for the night. All night we heard the incessant roar of the guns blazing away for all they were worth. Towards " Wipers " and, indeed, for many miles to the north, the sky was lit up with the flashes of artillery fire, Verey lights and rockets—only a few hours had to run now before zero. For our part we took the wise precaution of turning in as quickly as possible ; one never knew the moment that orders might come to shift a stage nearer the battle line.

Before dawn the attack had been launched from Woesten to Ypres, and before 11 o'clock that morning we heard some scraps of news from the line. One report said all objectives had been captured and our troops had broken through ; another, that the French Army was advancing through Houlthoust Forest—all equally untrue. Later in the day we got word, officially, that the attack was successful along the army front, and that in nearly every case the final objectives had been reached. This was good news, but our spirits sank considerably at the change in the weather. Our worst enemy in this stage of an attack was rain, and down it came, as it often had done before, on zero day. The result of the bad weather setting in was to hold up the attack for a week, which was all in favour of the enemy. Within a few hours the forward zone was little better than a quagmire of water-logged shell holes, a sea of mud and water in a land of absolute desolation.

Before nightfall we got instructions to move forward to an area just south of Vlambertinghe. A more disagreeable march it would be difficult to imagine. Rain came down steadily all night and the darkness was intense. It was only with difficulty that we found our location, and when we did the disappointment was very great. Soaked to the skin and thoroughly worn out, we discovered a bare field was our reward. Not even a trench or a hut to shelter in for the night. More by good luck than by good staff-work the men fixed up bivouacs out of their mackintosh sheets, but these hastily improvised shelters gave little or no protection against the elements. For the second time in our adventures the C.O. was forced to sleep under the mess cart, but even this luxury was not an enviable one.

The next morning we found ourselves completely nonplussed for ways and means to cook the breakfasts. Rain was still falling and the cold was intense. Our last hope was the sight of the Brigade Major who gave the C.O. the option of moving back to the huts we had vacated. The C.O. took advantage of the offer, and nobody was sorry to see the last of that field. To add to our discomfort the previous evening we came in for the unpleasant experience of being shelled with incendiary shells.

It was not until the 6th August that we finally moved into the front system, and took over from the 8th Inniskillings.   At 10 p.m. we marched up through Ypres, and after a most tiring walk through shell holes and the *débris* of the uncleared battle-field we took over the front line, or better described as a line of shell holes—the limit of the preliminary attack on the 31st July.

The exact location of the outpost line would be impossible to define, but as near as possible, the forward posts ran roughly through Frost House, that is to say, about 400 yards north-west of Frezenberg-Low Farm, and thence to the Hauebeck at a point 50 yards south of the southern limits of the old German S.P., known as Pommern Castle.   Beck House (a strongly fortified concrete pillbox) lay about 150 yards in front of the left centre of the battalion, and was held by the enemy with several machine-guns.   Practically, all the ruined farms in the Boche area had been turned into strongholds of reinforced concrete, which made the problem of attack much more difficult, as it meant the artillery could not deal with them all.   From inside these emplacements the enemy could spray us with machine-gun fire with comparative safety to himself.

In taking over the dispositions from the unit the C.O. was obliged to hold the sector with all four companies in the line.   Such a necessity was, of course, due to the weak state of our strength (19 officers and 472 other ranks) and partly owing to the length of front taken over.   A possibility was always likely that the enemy might attempt a counter-attack to regain some of the ground he had lost in the previous fortnight.   The inclemency of the weather and the heavy state of the ground made such a contingency unlikely, but the C.O. could not afford to take any risks.

Battalion Headquarters took over the occupation of Square Farm, which had many advantages had it not been so badly strafed by the Hun.   Apparently, it had previously been used by the enemy as an aid post, judging from the elaborate way in which the dug-outs were fitted up.   Strongly concreted inside and with a " burster " of five feet of reinforced cement on top, it seemed unlikely that a shell could penetrate through.   At any rate, during the C.O.'s occupation it was put to some very severe tests, and despite the enemy's attempts to demolish the building, it escaped with just a few slabs knocked off here and there.   The advantages to the headquarters outweighed the unpleasantness of the situation when the following facts are explained.   From the veranda an excellent view could be obtained of the enemy's defences.   With the exception of our own front line—in a dip— Ibernia Farm, Delva Farm, Zevencote, Coffee Farm, Hill 37 and Zonnebeke were clearly visible.   The configuration of the ground was such that the area was exceptionally free from obstruction by hedges and trees.   (No doubt the gunners had something to say to this.) A good well a few yards from the door was another useful acquisition.

Our experiences in the line from a tactical point of view are not important, nevertheless it was the most uncomfortable time the battalion had ever gone through on active service. All day, and at intervals during the night, the Hun artillery kept up an intermittent barrage fire on our sector. From dawn till dusk the troops forward of Square Farm were unable to move owing to the vigilance of the snipers and machine-guns ; this meant there was no intercourse whatsoever, during daylight, between Companies and Battalion Headquarters—in fact, between platoons and companies the position was almost as bad. Men had to sit tight in water-logged shell holes until it was dark enough to move about unobserved. Indeed, Square Farm fared nearly as badly, for it was used by the enemy as a target for the calibration of his artillery.

The C.O., in one of his letters to Brigade Headquarters, says : " This place reminds me of the Brickstack at Wytschaete. It " gets shelled all day and every day." Another nasty trick of the Boche was to strafe the Frezenberg Ridge and the tracks at odd hours in the hopes of catching working parties.

The intense artillery barrage put down by the enemy along the Divisional front on the night of the 7th was the cause of some alarm. From 8-55 p.m. onwards for over an hour the enemy's shells poured in in quick succession. No infantry action followed on our front, but it was understood that a raid had been attempted on one of the units on our right. To us the shoot did very little harm chiefly due to the inaccuracy of the German fire on our front posts.

Lieutenant T. H. Shaw and Sergeant Carroll were reported missing the next morning. At the time it was assumed they had lost their bearings in the dark and walked into the German lines by accident ; this theory was evidently incorrect, as they were never heard of again.

On the night of the 10th-11th August the battalion was relieved by the 2nd Royal Irish Regiment, and moved back to Toronto Camp, about three-quarters of a mile south-west of Brandhoek. For a change we were not asked to march, but entrained near the asylum in Ypres about midnight. The railway transport back to Brandhoek was a boon, for the men were dead beat from want of sleep and exposure.

Needless to say, the first day in reserve billets was spent in getting cleaned up. Hardly a rifle or Lewis gun was fit to fire after those four days of wet and mud. Even our clothes were caked from head to foot.

The ensuing three days were spent preparing equipment and

fixing details for the attack. It was the continuation of the offensive commenced along the army front on 31st July. The general idea was now to capture the Langemarck-Gheluvelt objectives—for convenience referred to as the " Green " line and the " Dotted Red " line. On the front to be attacked by the 16th (Irish) Division, the 49th Infantry Brigade were allotted the northern sector and the 48th Brigade the southern. The 47th Infantry Brigade formed the Divisional Reserve. In our Brigade Operation Orders dated the 14th August, the tasks of the units were detailed as follows :—

" The attack on the ' Green ' and ' Dotted Red ' lines will be " made by the 7th Royal Inniskilling Fusiliers on the left, and the " 8th Royal Inniskilling Fusiliers on the right. . . . There will " be a pause of twenty minutes on the ' Green ' line.

" As soon as the ' Red Dotted ' line has been captured, a line " of posts will be pushed out as far as the barrage will permit. . . . "   . . .   The 2nd Royal Irish Regiment will be in Brigade " reserve.

" At zero hour companies of the 2nd Royal Irish will advance " from their assembly positions and occupy the trenches vacated " by the assaulting battalions from D.25, A.80.05 to D.19, C.60.70, " with a post at Beck Ho. One company will remain in the " assembly position on the ' Blue ' line.

" Battalion Headquarters, 2nd Royal Irish Regiment, will move " to Square Farm when that of the 7th Inniskillings leaves for " Delva Farm."

The above is an extract from the general plan of the orders issued by the G.O.C. (Brigadier-General Leveson Gower). Various addenda and appendices were also issued regarding aircraft, artillery and communications to ensure the necessary cohesion of all arms.

On the evening of the 14th-15th August the battalion moved forward into its preparatory positions for the attacks. Our strength in *personnel* had been greatly minimised since we first came into this area, partly from the casualties we had sustained between the 6th and 10th of the month, and partly owing to an unusually heavy toll of trench fever. Our strength with us in the line amounted to 19 officers (including Battalion Headquarters) and 472 other ranks. About 5 officers and 100 other ranks remained behind with Echelon " B." Most of the companies going into action had no senior W.O.'s or N.C.O.'s ; the C.O. was left minus an adjutant and a signal officer. Captain E. H. Hester took over the duties of adjutant from this date, and Second-Lieutenant C. W. Fawkes acted as his assistant. Major R. G. Kerr, M.C., remained with " B " Echelon, and Captain V. H. Parr, M.C., came in as second-in-command. The companies were commanded as

follows :—" A " Company—Captain C. N. B. Walker ; " B "
Company—Captain D. H. Morton ; " C " Company—Captain
A. F. C. Graves ; " D " Company—Captain H. W. Ruddock.

On taking over the sector, " A " and " C " Companies held the
northern portion of the battalion frontage as occupied by " The
Seventh " between the 6th and 10th inst. ; the southern portion
was taken over by " The Eighth." Support companies remained
in the old German 2nd Line, and Battalion Headquarters returned
to Square Farm. The above dispositions remained in force until
the following evening, when the battalion formed up on its assembly
positions.

In forming up for the attack, " C " Company stood fast and
" A " Company was relieved by a company of the 7/8th Royal
Irish Fusiliers, and moved into a position behind " C " Company.
" B " and " D " Companies came up from the old German support
line, and passing Square Farm about 10-30 p.m. they took up
positions on the northern bank of the Hanebeek in continuation
of the line held by the other two companies, and at the same time
linking up as far as possible with the 9th R.I.F. on the left flank
(Ulster Division). Strictly speaking, the line adopted by our left
company was within the 36th Division boundary, but special
permission was granted for the intrusion so as to simplify our
advance, there being streams between us and the " Green " line
which might have impeded our advance.

A message from Brigade Headquarters about 11 p.m. fixed zero
hour at 4-45 o'clock in the morning. The second-in-command
distributed the information to companies verbally so as to ensure
no mistake being made.

During the night the enemy kept up a slow rate of artillery
fire, and at uncertain times swept our lines with machine-gun
fire. Our guns were also busy preparing the way for our advance
in the morning. The hostile action caused us some irritation,
and a certain amount of unavoidable delay was caused in taking
up our positions. At the moment the climatic conditions were
quite sufficient impediment to our progress without being shelled
at intervals. Every step taken meant sinking inches deep in the
mud. Under the circumstances the preliminary arrangements
were as thorough as could be expected, and by 2-30 a.m. the C.O.
had received a report from all company commanders stating they
were fixed up ready for zero.

At 4-45 a.m., in the grey light of dawn, the battle opened. The
barrage came down from our guns with perfect accuracy, but the
enemy replied within a minute with an equally powerful weight
of shell fire. Companies got well away before the Hun barrage
had fallen, and by zero, plus five, they had rushed Beck House
and the lone machine-gun emplacement on the left.

By 5-55 a.m. it was clearly visible from Square Farm that the troops had reached their allotted position on the " Green " line, and that the troops on the left were also going strong. To the right the situation did not appear to be quite so satisfactory, but it was impossible to form an opinion owing to the clouds of smoke hanging over the battlefield ; nevertheless, Beck House having been captured, the C.O. wired to the Brigade, stating : " Attack " going strong ; A.A.A. Beck House taken ; A.A.A. my men " going well."

On examining the ground with the aid of field-glasses at 5-50 a.m. the troops on the left (36th Division) appeared to be still making progress, but not quite so rapidly as at first. As far as one could see from Square Farm they were apparently up to Gallipoli Farm. The battalion itself were through Delva Farm, but the 8th Inniskillings seemed to be held up by machine-gun fire somewhere in the vicinity of Borry Farm. Some batches of walking wounded were coming down from the line, and from all reports the attack was progressing well, except for the enemy's machine-gun fire, which they said had caused severe casualties.

Between 7 and 7-45 a.m., the C.O. received several messages, including one from the 8th Inniskillings, to say they were held up by heavy machine-gun fire. One from Captain V. H. Parr, M.C., stated that Delva Farm had been captured, and that " B " Company were consolidating about 50 yards to the north of it ; emphasis, however, was laid on the fact that the " mopping up " had not been satisfactory, and that there was a lot of sniping going on behind our lines. The difficulties of the situation were to a great extent enhanced by the fact that there was no direct communication to anywhere forward. All despatches were delivered by orderly, which took a considerable amount of time.

The C.O. was satisfied that the situation at Borry Farm was obscure, and must at all costs be cleared up. To do this he ordered Major Scott, 2nd R.I.R., to send a company to deal with the situation in that place. This attempt was not successful, being handicapped for want of adequate artillery support.

A message from Delva, about 8 a.m., implied that the division on the left had been forced to retire, but at the time it was mere rumour ; nothing to that effect had been received from the flanks or from our own Brigade Headquarters.

Having roughly considered the operation from the point of view of an observer at Battalion Headquarters, let us now turn to what concerns us more—the actual trend of events with regard to the front system or, at any rate, as much as one can piece together from the stories of the survivors of the battle. No doubt, each officer, N.C.O. and man has a version of his own of what occurred, but with that we are not concerned. Individuals

THE CLOTH HALL, YPRES—1917.

attached to small units can only see what happens in their own sphere, and can therefore only contribute a small share in making up the narrative. Events, which to some may seem of paramount importance are, as a general rule, of little consequence in summing up the situation as a whole.

Captain V. H. Parr, M.C., to whom the C.O. entrusted the responsibility of establishing an advanced Battalion Headquarters at Delva Farm, accompanied the assaulting waves throughout the advance, and the report which he made to Colonel Young throws more light on the situation than any other eye-witness can relate. It was for his coolness, courage and good leadership throughout the battle that he was subsequently awarded the Distinguished Service Order.

The following is an extract from this officer's statement :—

" At zero hour I was in the front-line trench, about D.19, c. 50.40, " and behind me was the Battalion Headquarters party under " the command of Captain Hester. From this party I detailed " two runners to remain with me throughout the attack. My " idea at this time was to leave Captain Hester in command of the " advance party (signallers, snipers, runners, etc.), so that I should " be free to leave them at a moment's notice in case I should be " required elsewhere.

" At zero hour we advanced about 100 yards to the left of " ' A ' Company's third wave, so as to be clear of our own trench. " We made straight on for Delva Farm. As we passed Beck House " I noticed that it had already been captured by our men, and " some prisoners were taken. We continued on our way and " crossed the Zonnebeke at a point about midway between Pommern " Castle and Beck House (D.19, d.00.70). There was no difficulty " in crossing the stream, but a line of wire entanglements on the " right bank, which had escaped our artillery bombardment, " caused us some difficulty.

" On arrival at the southern end of Iberian Strong Point " I noticed there was considerable rifle fire going on, and in " the next few minutes my signalling sergeant was hit by a bullet. " I ordered the snipers who were with me to advance to the " eastern edge of the Strong Point, and take up a position until I " rejoined them. As far as I could see, there did not appear to " be any of our troops in Ibernia, though it was then 6-30 a.m. " Shortly after we noticed a German looking out of one of the " dug-outs. I arranged that all dug-outs in this vicinity should " be throughly searched. In one we found twenty Germans " and two machine-guns. At first they hesitated to come out, " but on being threatened with a revolver they came out unarmed. " This particular pill-box was a concrete machine-gun emplace- " ment facing in the direction of Frezenburg. In all, we searched

" about three dug-outs, and got forty prisoners and three machine
" guns.   At the time I could not spare any of my men as escort,
" so I ordered the prisoners to report at Square Farm, which I
" understand now they did.   As a precaution I took the breech
" blocks from the machine-guns and threw them into a shell hole.

" The clearing of these dug-outs had caused some delay to our
" advance, so we proceeded straight away in the direction of
" Delva Farm.   When I came to Delva I noticed that ' B ' Com-
" pany were extended in shell craters about twenty yards in front
" of the farm.   Captain D. H. Morton had been wounded during
" the attack, and was lying in a shell hole close by.   This officer
" explained the situation to me.   Unfortunately, at this juncture
" I lost my note-book, so am unable to give any idea of the time.
" I imagine it was about 5 a.m. when I got to Delva Farm.   Even
'on my arrival there, the position was under intense machine-
'gun fire from the south, which was growing steadily more
'persistent—I fancied this came from Bremen Redoubt.

" My first idea was to locate ' D ' Company, and I sent a runner
" to find their whereabouts.   In a short time Captain H. W.
" Ruddock came back personally to report to me.   He then
" told me that he had reached a line 150 yards in front of Delva
" Farm, that his casualties were slight up to this, but that he
" was under very intense machine-gun fire, and not in touch
" with any troops on either flank.

" Up to this time there was a persistent rumour that the unit
" on our left had retired, but I tried to believe it was only wounded
" men going back to the aid posts.

" By watching Hill 35 and the ground in front of it through
" my glasses, I became convinced that the troops on our left
" were, in fact, retiring.   As a result of this I ordered Lieutenant
" N. H. Woods, M.C. (now in command of ' B ' Company), to
" form a defensive flank facing north-east.   At the same time
" I got in touch with a platoon of 'A' Company, under Lieutenant
" W. T. Smythe, on the right.   The latter told me that, as far
" as he could discover, there were no troops on his right flank.
" I ordered him to stand fast, and be prepared to support ' D '
" Company, or to form a defensive flank.

" At this stage I sent two orderlies with a report to battalion
" headquarters (Square Farm) on the situation.   This report I
" duplicated by sending a pigeon message to say that our position
" was critical unless either or both our flanks were re-established.
" Up to this, the signal section with me had failed to get in
" touch with anyone, owing to loss of *personnel* and insufficient
" equipment.

" From where I was Square Farm was distinctly visible, and
'· was being heavily shelled, but my attention was now directed

" to three enemy aeroplanes flying very low over our lines. These
" machines circled over our heads for about twenty minutes,
" firing bursts into the line. Several casualties were caused
" near me by this action.

" At 8-30 a.m. I got word that we were being counter-attacked,
" so I went out in front to ascertain if this was true. I saw the
" enemy were advancing towards 'D' Company, who were
" firing ' rapid,' and appeared to have the situation well in hand.
" Another message came when I was there from 'B' Company,
" in which I was informed that Lieutenant Woods had been
" killed. I went across to where he had been, and on arrival
" I saw the Germans advancing from a northerly direction,
" with apparently Hill 35 and Delva Farm as their objectives.
" When I first saw them they were advancing in two lnes,
" at about five paces interval ; their right flank was almost on
" Hill 35, which appeared to be undefended, and they were then
" only 400 yards away from where we stood. I shouted to the
" men who were near me to open fire, but my voice did not carry
" very far.

" It was evident to me now that the main attack was coming
" from the direction of Gallipoli, that the enemy were in pos-
" session of Hill 35, and that the only chance of saving the battalion,
" and possibly the brigade, lay in forming a defensive flank facing
" north, from Delva Farm to Ibernia. I assumed at the time
" that there was a company of Royal Irish Fusiliers in Ibernia,
" with two platoons holding a position in front of that point,
" and I hoped that I would re-form 'B' Company on the
" plan suggested above.

" Before leaving Delva Farm I told Captain Hester to hold
" on to the farm with the troops at his disposal, and thereby
" protect the left flank of 'D' Company. Having briefly
" explained the situation, I went with my runner (Lance-Corporal
" McHale) after 'B' Company. Within the next fifteen minutes
" I succeeded in collecting various parties of stragglers, in all
" amounting to about forty men, and I endeavoured with these
" to re-form a line. Unfortunately, the casualties had been
" so heavy that it was difficult to find any N.C.O.'s to put in
" charge of the men.

" When I reached Ibernia I could find no organised body of
" R.I.F., but, with the assistance of Captain Sargint we suc-
" ceeded in restoring the situation for a while. The enemy's
" barrage fire was very intense at this time, and severe casualties
" were sustained. It was then that Captain Sargint, my runner
" and myself were all hit.

" It still appeared to me that one well-organised platoon would
" have turned the scale. I could now see the enemy in large

" numbers on Hill 35, and to me there did not seem any limit
" to the amount of ground over which they could advance, at
" least until they reached the line held by the Royal Irish Regi-
" ment at Bavaria Farm.   From where I stood I could see a
" large number of men round Beck House, and I thought the
" best course to take was to re-form these.   .   .   .   I got them
" into the old German line just behind Beck House, and ordered
" them to stop all stragglers and absorb them into their strength.
" As far as I could make out, our old front line was strongly
" held by the Royal Irish Regiment, and I wished to tell them
" how the land lay, but realised that I could not explain such
" a situation on paper.   On thinking the matter over, I decided
" the position we now held was of no value compared to the
" importance of informing the supporting troops as to the situa-
" tion, so I ordered my party to retire on the old front line.   I
" warned each man that it was very important to move slowly
" back, and keep his required distance, as the machine-gun fire
" was very heavy.   When I reached our old front line I was
" surprised to find that the line was strongly held by Inniskillings
" and Royal Irish.   After an l our I came across an officer (I
" don't know his name).   I put him in charge of that portion of
" the line, and told him that it must be held at all costs.   I then
" returned to Square Farm and made my report to Colonel Young."

Such were the incidents that happened on our front on the
16th August, 1917, at least as much as this short narrative can
record.   In the afternoon, about 1-30 o'clock, the first message
since the commencement of the attack was received from brigade
headquarters.   It made no reference to any previous reports
Colonel Young had sent in, but was merely a direct order to
capture Borry Farm at all costs.   This order was cancelled later
in the afternoon, when the C.O. pointed out that the scheme
had little or no chance of success.

At 3-15 p.m. a message came from the 8th Inniskillings, stating
they were holding a line 100 yards west of Borry Farm, and that
this farm was causing them casualties from snipers and machine-
guns.   Eventually, this line turned out to be held by both
the 7th and 8th Inniskillings.   Second-Lieutenant A. H. H.
Armstrong, of " The Seventh," coming in from it *via* Beck House,
said he entered the farm and saw numerous wounded, both of
our own troops and the Germans.   He thought the time was
then about 3-15 p.m.

That evening the brigade was relieved, and eventually moved
back to Vlambertinghe on the 17th.   On the 18th the C.O. took over
temporary command of the 49th Infantry Brigade, and Second-
Lieutenant A. H. H. Armstrong commanded the battalion until
Major R. G. Kerr, M.C., assumed command back in Godewaersvelde.

SQUARE FARM

ENTERING YPRES from SOUTH WEST 1917

L'ÉCOLE - YPRÈS 1917

On the 22nd August the battalion moved off by train at 4-50 a.m. for down south, arriving at Miraumont (Somme Area) at 12-50 p.m., from whence they marched to Achiet-le-Petit, and the following day the amalgamation took place with the 8th Royal Inniskilling Fusiliers.

Two special orders were published by Colonel Young, D.S.O., on the 21st and 23rd August, 1917, respectively, and require no further explanation. They read as follows :—

" Officers and men of the ' Fighting ' Seventh Inniskillings :
" The more one learns of the Battle of the 16th August at Ypres, ·
" when you advanced fearlessly against strong opposition as
" only true Inniskillings can, and captured all your objectives,
" including Hill 35, Ibernia Farm, Delva Farm, right up to the
" Langemarck-Gheluvelt line, and hung on there until forced
" back by overwhelming numbers, both your flanks having long
" since been exposed, the more pride one should feel in belonging
" to such a body of men. You have nobly upheld the honour
" and traditions of your battalion and parent regiment, and
" by your courage and devotion to duty won fresh laurels for
" them. Our casualties were very severe. Out of 20 officers
" and 472 men, who went into action, only 7 officers and 114
" other ranks came out with the battalion. All ranks must now
" endeavour to re-form and organise the battalion so that we
" shall be ready when called upon."

" SPECIAL ORDER.

" 23/8/17.

" Officers and Other Ranks of the old 7th and 8th Battalions
" of the Royal Inniskilling Fusiliers are from this date amalga-
" mated as one battalion. As such, they must continue to accrue
" fresh honours for their parent regiment. Both battalions
" have records of which any battalion in the British Army would
" be proud to possess. Let it now be the aim of all to win a name
" for the combined battalions which will, if possible, even surpass
" the record of either.

" (Signed) H. N. YOUNG, Lieut.-Colonel."

EPILOGUE

It seems a pity that I am unable to continue the history of the battalion up to the time of the Armistice. On the other hand, it is only by the help of a few officers that I managed to record the deeds of " The Seventh " so far as I have done.

The obvious question to ask is, what subsequently happened to the battalion and all the remaining officers and men ?

Shortly after the amalgamation with the 8th Inniskillings, Lieutenant-Colonel A. J. Walkey assumed command, which position he held up to the 21st March, 1918, when he was wounded, and the Division was withdrawn from the line, having suffered most severely in the German offensive.

Only a few of the original battalion were still serving after this offensive. Major V. H. Parr, D.S.O., M.C., was wounded and a prisoner of war, and Captain C. H. Stainforth, M.C., was severely wounded and invalided home. A few months later Major R. G. Kerr, M.C., was killed whilst attached to the Royal Irish Fusiliers, and lastly, our gallant commanding officer, Lieutenant-Colonel H. N. Young, D.S.O., fell on 25th October, 1918. Our late C.O. won a bar to his D.S.O. in June, 1918, also the Croix de Guerre avec palme, and the Italian silver medal for valour. He was killed near Le Cateau in command of the Sherwood Foresters, after a most distinguished career as a soldier and Commanding Officer.

The last to leave the battalion of the original members was the Quartermaster, Captain W. Reid, M.C., D.C.M. He remained with the 7/8th until after the presentation of the King's Colours at Boulogne on the 29th August, 1919. On that parade Brigadier-General F. W. Ramsay, C.B., C.M.G., D.S.O. (late G.O.C. 48th Infantry Brigade), presented the colours after their consecration, and said :

" I cannot but express to you how much I appreciate the

" great honour which I have had to-day in presenting to you the
" King's Colours after two and a half years' fighting alongside
" you in the 16th (Irish) Division, after witnessing your gallant
" actions in the war, and your devotion to duty through all the
" long years of weary trench warfare, and especially after all
" your battalion did for me in the memorable Battle of Ginchy.
" I feel there is no one to whom this privilege could have given
" greater pleasure, and I assure you there is no one who has any
" greater sympathy or greater admiration for the Irish soldier.
   " You commenced a most glorious and honourable career
" on the 27th April, 1916, when, in company with my Dublin
" Fusiliers, you were instrumental in the defeat of the Bavarians
" just west of Hulluch. It was you who captured Leuze Wood,
" on the Somme, in September, 1916, though the credit of it was
" given to another division. On the 9th September you were
" placed under my command, and assisted me in the capture of
" the village of Ginchy and Telegraph Hill, a stronghold which
" had resisted the attacks of no less than three British divisions.
" Although the brigades on either flank of you failed to leave
" their trenches, you gallantly fought your way on and reached
" your final objective. In spite of both of your flanks being
" exposed, and in spite of repeated counter-attacks, you held
" your ground until relieved by the Grenadiers and Welsh Guards
" at midnight. In this action you showed all the finest fighting
" qualities of the Irish soldier ; you made the name of the Irish
" Division, and you made history for Ireland. This position was
" the key to all the future operations on the Somme, and was
" the cause of their final success.
   " Your next exploit was on the Messines-Wytschaete Ridge,
" where you captured the high ground in the wood just north
" of the Hospice. This has since and is now called ' Inniskilling
" Wood.' Under your very gallant and able leader, Colonel
" H. N. Young, D.S.O., you distinguished yourselves at Friesen-
" burg, and did all that was possible in a desperate situation.
" In the Battle of Cambrai you assisted my brigade in the capture
" of the line near Bullecourt.
   " In the great German attack in March, 1918, when, under
" cover of mist the enemy were able to enter our lines, you
" gallantly fought all day in the village of Roncoy, and, as we
" heard afterwards from prisoners, your men in the strong points
" were still holding out next day at mid-day, although entirely
" surrounded by the enemy. As you have added to the glorious
" traditions of your regiment in action, so you can, by loyalty,
" by kindness to those who are down on their luck, by smartness
" in appearance and carriage, by fearlessly acting on the side of
" law and order, continue to maintain the strong traditions of

(*Photo kindly lent by Capt. G. O. F. Alley, M.C., R.A.M.C.*)

THE LAST OF THE ORIGINAL "SEVENTH" IN MARCH 1918.

" your regiment. I feel sure that the same spirit of good feeling
" and good sense which has helped you to achieve such great
" things in this war will bring to you in the future, peace and
" prosperity."

The following is an extract from a letter written by Major-
General Sir W. B. Hickie, K.C.B. :—

" To the Officers, N.C.O.'s and Men of the 7/8th Battalion
" Royal Inniskilling Fusiliers. I have asked General Ramsey to
" convey to all ranks of this very distinguished battalion my
" congratulations on this day when they are to receive the colours
" from his hands. It is a great regret that I cannot be present
" myself, and I am much complimented and gratified at the
" invitation I have received. The Inniskilling Fusiliers played
" a most distinguished part in the great war. During the two
" and a-half years for which I commanded the 16th (Irish) Division,
" the ' Skins ' never failed. I shall always remember with pride
" their gallantry in battle, their devotion to duty in the long
" months of trench warfare, and their smartness and discipline
" in camp and in quarters. I remember all the good and gallant
" soldiers who have given their lives to their country ; all the
" maimed and wounded ; men whose efforts helped to build up
" the fame which is symbolised by these colours ; and lastly, to
" all old Inniskilling Fusiliers, present and absent, who have
" contributed by services to enhance the glories and uphold the
" traditions of the Royal Inniskilling Fusiliers, I send my greetings
" and congratulations. They hand over a great record and a
" glorious past."

It would be quite impossible to conclude before paying a tribute
to all those who helped and looked after the battalion so well
when they were serving in France. First, to Mrs. Hughes, and
those who worked continuously, sending out and making comforts
for our men in the trenches ; and secondly, to those who so gener-
ously subscribed to the battalion memorial fund. Though the
latter is still in abeyance, and nothing definite has been decided
on by the committee, we may rest assured that whatever form it
may take, it will be treasured for all time as a reminder of
those gallant band of Inniskillings who gave their lives for God,
King, Country and Regiment.

> " For one a little cross of deal,
> For one the age-enduring tree ;
> Yet each frail, faltering flesh did feel
> In hands and feet, the wounding steel.
> Each died that mankind might be free ;
> Each gave a life for you and me."
>
> JOSEPH LEE (*Ballads of B ttle*).

PLAN
of Bn. Cemetery, 7th Royal Inniskilling Fusiliers,
Philosophe East, —— Loos Salient.

Gate

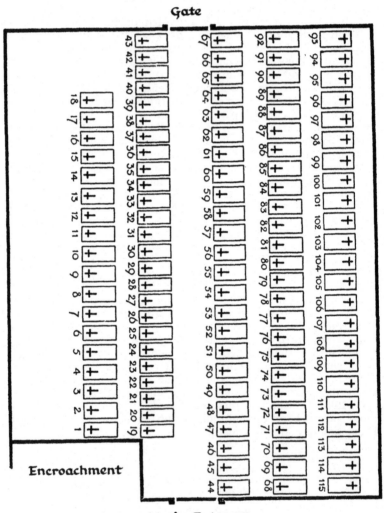

Encroachment

Main Entrance .

KEY

to the

BATTALION CEMETERY

at

PHILOSOPHE EAST

(LOOS SALIENT)

---◆---

ROW I.

NO. OF GRAVE ON DESIGN	REGI- MENTAL NO.	RANK	NAME		CAUSE OF DEATH
1.	27030	Private	Gallagher, P.	—	Died of wounds
2.	22732	Private	Millar, H.	—	do.
3.	16511	Sergeant	McMurray, F. W.	—	do.
4.	13746	Private	Morgan, M.	—	do.
5.	23035	Private	Johnston, T.	—	do.
6.	23668	Private	Little, P.	—	do.
7.	23352	Private	Thompson, A.	—	do.
8.	28848	Private	Poller, J.	—	Killed in action
9.	23871	Private	Johnson, D.	—	do.
10.	22992	Private	Gallagher, D.	—	do.
11.	28621	Private	Mulholland, J.	—	Died of wounds
12.	23757	Private	Kelly, P.	—	do.
13.	25138	Private	Anderson, W.	—	Killed in action
14.	26893	Private	Arthur, J.	—	do.
15.	24018	Private	Sheffield, W. J.	—	do.
16.	17964	C.S.M.	Carey, W. C.	—	Died of wounds
17.	20141	Private	McConnachie, R.	—	Killed in action
18.	24074	Private	Gilliland, S. J.	—	do.

ROW II.

19.	26509	Private	Best, J.	—	Killed in action
20.		2/Lieut.	N. H. Collins	—	Died of wounds
21.	25290	Private	Porter, P.	—	Killed in action
22.	26452	Private	Moloney, M.	—	do.
23.	23032	Private	Jackson, W.	—	do.
24	24738	Private	Hanna, P.	—	Died of wounds
25.	23755	Private	McCarron, M.	—	Killed in action
26.	23671	Private	Lee, J.	—	do.
27.	23354	Private	Kyle, A.	—	do.
28.	24914	Private	Byrne, G.	—	Died of wounds
29.	23574	Private	McCrossan, B.	—	Killed in action

NO. OF GRAVE ON DESIGN	REGIMENTAL NO.	RANK	NAME	CAUSE OF DEATH
30.	20431	Private	McConkey, J.	Killed in action
31.	27549	Private	McCarthy, J.	do.
32.	23777	Corporal	Clinton, F.	do.
33.		2/Lieut.	N. D. Trimble	Died of wounds
		(8th Royal Inniskillling Fusiliers)		
34.	21259	Corporal	Boardman, D. P.	Killed in action
35.	23438	Private	Lawson, H.	Died of wounds
36.	27546	Private	Murphy, A.	Killed in action
37.	26640	Private	Connors, P.	do.
38.		2/Lieut.	F. A. W. Milligan	Died of wounds
39.	26954	Private	Tosh, A.	Killed in action
40.	27700	Private	Murphy, A.	Died of wounds
41.	22326	L/Cpl.	Gallocher, C.	Killed in action
42.	13410	C.S.M.	Taylor, W.	do.
43.	23075	Private	O'Rourke, P.	do.

ROW III.

44.	27704	Private	Kavanagh, M.	Died of wounds
45.	24521	Private	Hobson, —.	Killed in action
46.	28625	Corporal	Templeton, J.	do.
47.	16548	Sergeant	Leslie, J.	do.
48.	28634	Private	McHaffie, J.	do.
49.	27041	Private	Wilson, W.	do.
50.	20273	Private	Kelly, M.	do.
51.	14776	Private	Cornthwaite, H. C.	do.
52.	25302	Private	Gallagher, M.	do.
53.	24892	Private	Donnelly, P.	do.
54.	26983	Private	O'Connor, B.	do.
55.	27063	Private	Cassidy, W.	do.
56.	20502	Private	O'Neill, J.	do.
57.	25537	Private	Harte, T.	do.
58.	25289	Private	McHugh, M.	Died of wounds
59.	23132	Private	Sheridan, J.	Killed in action
60.	23587	Private	Harkin, A.	do.
61.	28650	Private	Hill, W.	Died of wounds
62.	26458	Private	Ferrey, P.	Killed in action
63.	An unknown British Soldier			do.
64.	23138	Corporal	Wilson, T.	Died of wounds
65.	27475	Private	McManus, F.	do.
66.	26293	Private	Doloughan, F.	Killed in action
67.	An unknown British Soldier			do.

ROW IV.

68.	26477	Private	Storan, E.	Killed in action
69.	28695	L/Corpl.	Ramsey, A.	do.
70.	26979	Private	Dunwoody, J.	do.
71.	23433	Private	McManus, P.	do.
72.	22793	Private	Crown, J.	Died of wounds
73.	20300	Corporal	Parry, R.	Killed in action

NO. OF GRAVE ON DESIGN	REGI- MENTAL NO.	RANK	NAME		CAUSE OF DEATH
74.	26463	L/Corpl.	Walsh, P.	......	Killed in action
75.	22851	Private	Woods, J.	......	do.
76.	23673	Private	Corrigan, M.	......	do.
77.	27719	Private	Glennon, T.	......	do.
78.	23894	Private	Gallagher, W.	......	do.
79.	22867	Private	Fitzgerald, E.	......	do.
80.	3368	Private	Kearney, F. J.	......	do.
81.	24335	Private	Coyle, J.	......	do.
82.	23577	Private	Curtis, B.	......	do.
83.	28678	Sergeant	Pearson, T.	......	do.
84.	23038	Private	Gallagher, J.	......	do.
85.	11924	Private	Gorman, H.	......	do.
86.	26952	Private	Regan, W.	......	do.
87.	28649	L/Corpl.	Murphy, M.	......	Died of wounds
88.	23973	Private	McCready, R.	......	Killed in action
89.	16522	L/Sergt.	Finnegan, P. P.	......	do.
90.	21305	Private	Gavigan, J.	......	do.
91.	24526	Corporal	McInally, J.	......	do.
92.	26658	Private	Cassidy, T.	......	do.

ROW V.

93.	24705	Private	McGrath, J.	......	Killed in action
94.	23667	Private	Shields, G.	......	Died of wounds
95.	17721	Private	McKinney, D.	......	Killed in action
96.	13672	Sergeant	Barrett, J.	......	Died of wounds
97.		2/Lieut.	B. Watson	......	do.
98.		2/Lieut.	J. S. Knox	......	do.
99.	28865	Private	Ryder, P.	......	Killed in action
100.	26514	Private	Maher, P.	......	Died of wounds
101.	6350	L/Corpl.	Tyrrell, B.	......	Killed in action
102.	26468	Private	Moriarty, M.	......	do.
103.	22505	Private	Brown, P.	......	do.
104.	27573	Private	Brady, P.	......	do.
105.	18305	Private	McIntosh, J.	......	do.
106.	13033	Private	Jamieson, A.	......	Died of wounds
107.	24747	Private	Spence, R.	......	Killed in action
108.	27563	Private	McIlherron, D.	......	Died of wounds
109.	27343	Private	Malley, D.	......	Killed in action
110.	24087	Private	Duffy, T.	......	do.
111.	13395	Sergeant	Christian, J.	......	do.
112.		*Captain	R. N. Murray	......	Died of wounds
113.	13419	Sergeant	Mulholland, W. J.	......	do.
114.	25968	Sergeant	Brennan, M.	......	Killed in action
115.	22634	Corporal	Gahan, R.	......	do.

* This grave was erected as a memorial. Captain R. N. Murray died of gas poisoning in a German field hospital as a prisoner of war on the 29th April, 1916.

I

THIS CROSS WAS ERECTED NEAR GINCHY TO THE
MEMORY OF THE 16TH (IRISH) DIVISION.

Appendix

—◆═╫·╫═◆—

Roll of Honour

The names of the officers mentioned are those who were on the strength of the 7th Battalion Royal Inniskilling Fusiliers at any time during the war, and who were killed serving with the unit or subsequently, up to the date of the Armistice. Regarding " other ranks," the names are given in alphabetical order of those who were killed prior to the amalgamation. In some cases names are included of those who were killed after August 26th, 1917—these belonged to the original " Seventh." Lack of data does not allow of the inclusion of those who were transferred to other units, and were killed in action in other regiments. The Roll in all cases includes killed in action, died of wounds, sickness or gas, and missing, believed killed.

Roll of Honour

OFFICERS.

Lieut.-Colonel H. N. Young, D.S.O., Royal Inniskilling Fusiliers.
Lieut.-Colonel A. D. Reid, D.S.O., (attached Royal Irish Rifles).

Major R. G. Kerr, M.C. (attached Royal Irish Fusiliers).

Captain W. H. Collis.
Captain R. N. Murray.
Captain J. Ritty, M.C.
Captain A. F. C. Graves.
Captain C. N. B. Walker.
Captain R. T. Sutton.
Captain E. Hester.

Lieutenant N. H. Woods, M.C.
Lieutenant T. H. Shaw
Lieutenant E J. McCormick (attached R.A.F.).

2/Lieutenant F. A. W. Milligan.
2/Lieutenant N. H. Collins.
2/Lieutenant F. S. Carroll.
2/Lieutenant B. Watson.
2/Lieutenant J. S. Knox.
2/Lieutenant J. R. Moore (Connaught Rangers).
2/Lieutenant W. Morgan.
2/Lieutenant C. A. Crowe.
2/Lieutenant D. W. Holmes.
2/Lieutenant G. Coombes, D.C.M., M.M. (Royal
    Irish Fusiliers.)
2/Lieutenant J. Collen (attached R.A.F.).
2/Lieutenant N. H. E. Linde.
2/Lieutenant T. J. Dalton.

WARRANT OFFICER (Class 1).

13133 A/Regt. Sergt.-Major R. Dolan, D.C.M.

OTHER RANKS.

REGIMENTAL NO.	RANK	NAME			DATE
3396	Private	Aiken, W. E.			9– 9-16
30129	Private	Allen, G. L.			7– 6-17
25412	Private	Anderson, C. E.			3– 4-16
25138	Private	Anderson, W.			5– 4-16
22981	L/Corpl.	Armstrong, W.			16– 8-17
26893	Private	Arthur, J.			6– 4-16
24742	Private	Bailey, T.			16– 8-17
13672	Sergeant	Barrett, J.			15– 6-16
12370	Private	Barrington, H.			16– 8-17
26493	Sergeant	Bell, C.			9– 9-16
24681	Private	Bell, H.			9– 5-17
43299	Private	Bell, T.			9– 9-16
26509	Private	Best, J.			27– 4-16
41801	Private	Bishop, G. H.			16– 8-17
9437	Corporal	Blakely, B.			9– 9-16
24234	Private	Blann, D.			16– 3-17
21259	Corporal	Boardman, D. P.			6– 4-16
29399	Private	Bogan, T. J.			16– 8-17
43187	Private	Bolger, N.			9-10-16
41663	Private	Bond, E. J.			17– 3-19
28682	Private	Bower, J. H.			9– 9-16
24960	Private	Boyle, P.			27– 4-16
28912	Private	Boyle, W.			21– 3-18
24964	Private	Boyne, J.			27– 4-16
27573	Private	Brady, P.			19– 7-16
26503	Private	Brady, T.			9– 9-16
43222	Private	Brazil, C.			16– 8-17
25968	Sergeant	Brennan, H. P.			30– 4-16
23139	Private	Brennan, M.			9– 9-16
21303	Private	Brogan, J.			9– 9-16
22505	Private	Brown, P.			6– 8-16
11981	Private	Browning, J.			25– 4-16
24687	Private	Buckley, J.			10– 6-17
25919	Private	Bunting, D.			14– 6-17
27566	Private	Burns, D.			31– 5-16
26930	Private	Burns, J.			2– 4-16
30111	Private	Burtenshaw, A.			7– 6-17
41836	Private	Butler, S.			23– 8-17
41231	Private	Butterworth, W.			16– 8-17
29537	Private	Byrne, F.			4-10-16
24914	Private	Byrne, G.			25– 4-16
41234	Private	Cairns, J.			31– 8-17
28880	Private	Campbell, P.			16– 8-17
17964	C.S.M.	Carey, W. C.			27– 4-16
20209	Sergeant	Carroll, S.			8– 8-17
3474	Private	Casey, F.			9– 9-16
27367	Private	Cassidy, M.			29– 7-16
26658	Private	Cassidy, T.			27– 4-16

REGIMENTAL NO.	RANK	NAME			DATE
27063	Private	Cassidy, W.			20– 5–16
23267	Private	Caulfield, D.			9– 9–16
43298	Private	Cowley, J.			9– 9–16
41791	Private	Champion, A.			16– 8–17
41163	Private	Choate, H.			16– 8–17
41807	Private	Chorley, J.			16– 8–17
13395	Sergeant	Christian, J.			25– 8–16
26031	Private	Clark, W.			27– 4–16
27547	Private	Clarkin, J.			27– 4–16
25107	Private	Clinton, M.			15– 5–17
23777	Corporal	Clinton, T.			19– 4–16
26329	Private,	Clucas, R.			27– 4–16
41724	Private	Cluett, H. F.			16– 8–17
22780	Corporal	Cochrane, C.			18– 6–16
19912	Private	Cogan, P.			21– 3–18
13437	Private	Coleman, S.			27– 4–16
30096	Private	Coles, J. W.			16– 8–17
41903	Private	Collings, T.			16– 8–17
25595	Private	Collins, A.			10– 9–16
27702	Private	Connell, P.			27– 4–16
27552	Private	Connor, D.			1– 4–17
26440	Private	Connors. P.			6– 4–16
4227	Private	Conroy, J.			19– 8–17
3230	Sergeant	Conway, A.			21– 3–18
41207	Private	Cookson, J.			13–10–17
41235	Private	Cookson, W.			7– 6–17
14776	Private	Cornthwaite, H. C.			27– 4–16
23673	Private	Corrigan, M.			27– 4–16
28450	Private	Costello, M. A.			7– 6–17
30179	Private	Cousens, A. A.			16– 8–17
24335	Private	Coyle, J.			27– 4–16
26920	Private	Criglington, R.			6– 3–16
28701	Private	Crowley, W.			9– 9–16
22795	Private	Crown, J.			28– 4–16
30301	Private	Crowson, S.			7– 6–16
26500	Private	Cunneen, J.			27– 4–16
26864	Private	Cunning, J.			21– 3–18
28633	Private	Curley, J.			16– 8–17
23517	Private	Curtis, B.			27– 4–16
41727	Private	Cutts, A.			16– 8–17
21100	Private	Daly, F.			16– 8–17
21304	Private	Daly, R.			30– 9–18
41789	Private	Darch, C.			16– 8–17
27703	Private	Daye, J.			27– 4–16
30328	Private	Diggle, A.			16– 8–17
21277	L/Corpl.	Docherty, T.			9– 9–16
26761	Private	Doherty, J.			21– 3–18
20425	Private	Doherty, M.			16–10–16
22736	Private	Doherty, P.			27– 4–16
26293	Private	Doloughan, F.			27– 4–16
43262	Private	Donnelly, J.			9– 9–16
24892	Private	Donnelly, P.			27– 4–16
28637	Private	Douglas, A.			16– 8–17
30302	Private	Drabble, J.			8– 8–17

REGIMENTAL NO.	RANK	NAME		DATE
29674	Sergeant	Drumm, J.		5- 6-17
26466	Private	Duddy, H.		27- 4-16
24087	Private	Duffy, T.		54- 8-16
26979	Private	Dunwoody, J.		27- 4-16
41730	Private	Dutton, H.		16- 8-17
30158	L/Corpl.	Edwards., L P		17- 6-17
43195	L/Corpl.	Evans, R.		16- 8-17
16667	Private.	Ezard, W.		6- 9-16
28509	Private	Felly, M.		9- 9-16
25582	Private	Fenton, W.		16- 8-17
26458	Private	Ferry, P.		3- 5-16
16522	Sergeant	Finngean, P. P.		28- 4-16
22867	Private	Fitzgerald, E.		28- 4-16
28807	Corporal	Foley, R. H.		16- 8-17
41809	Private	Fountain, G.		21- 3-18
25569	Private	Friele, P.		9- 9-16
29392	L/Corpl.	Gaffney, J.		9- 9-16
22634	Corporal	Gahan, P.		27- 4-16
21115	Private	Gallagher, C.		29- 4-16
22992	Private	Gallagher, D.		2- 4-16
23038	Private	Gallagher, J.		30- 4-16
25302	Private	Gallagher, M.		27- 4-16
27030	Private	Gallagher, P.		10- 3-16
23894	Private	Gallagher, W.		30- 4-16
22326	Private	Gallocher, C.		6- 4-16
18021	Private	Gartland, W.		27- 4-16
21305	Private	Gaviglan, J.		27- 4-16
22984	Private	Gibbons, G.		6- 4-16
24734	Private	Gilbey, J.		27- 4-16
25750	Private	Gill, J.		21-10-16
43202	Private	Gilligan, J.		6- 9-16
24074	Private	Gilliland, S. J.		5- 4-16
27719	Private	Glennon, T.		27- 4-16
30104	Private	Godden, W. G.		16- 8-17
13447	Corporal	Gordon, W.		8- 8-17
11924	Private	Gorman, H.		27- 4-16
26946	Private	Graham, W.		16- 8-17
41886	Private	Greenwood, C.		16- 8-17
43223	Private	Gribben, W.		16- 8-17
30150	Private	Grinstead, G. H.		16- 8-17
26897	Private	Guthrie, H.		21- 3-18
20321	Private	Hagan, H.		21- 3-18
27032	L/Corpl.	Haggerty, W.		16- 8-17
24738	Private	Hanna, P.		1- 6-16
24842	Corporal	Hanna, P.		27- 4-16
23587	Private	Harkin, A.		27- 4-16
26395	Private	Harkin, J.		9- 9-16
30193	Corporal	Harnell, W. J.		7- 6-17
25537	Private	Harte, T.		18- 5-16
41817	Private	Harwood, P. H.		9- 8-17
28037	Private	Haughney, C.		3- 7-18

REGIMENTAL NO.	RANK	NAME			DATE
41831	Private	Hayball, C.			16– 8–17
27712	Private	Hayden, G.			22– 4–16
41919	Private	Hazlehurst, C.			21– 3–18
30138	Private	Hedge, W.			16– 8–17
23978	Private	Henderson, P.			9– 9–16
19638	Private	Higginson, H.			9– 5–17
28650	Private	Hill, W.			27– 4–16
41733	Private	Hines, F.			16– 8–17
24521	Private	Hobson, M.			30– 4–16
41880	Private	Hobson, W. L.			15– 8–17
27699	Private	Holden, J.			16– 8–17
41167	Private	Honeyball, G. W. W.			16– 8–17
41652	Private	Hopkins, J. C.			21– 3–18
43283	Private	Horkin, P.			15– 9–16
16484	Private	Houston, F.			7– 9–16
41843	Private	Huggins, R. J.			3– 9–17
41239	Private	Hulme, F.			7– 6–17
41659	Private	Hutchings, W.			16 –8–17
23032	Private	Jackson, W.			20– 5–16
41736	Private	James, H.			16– 8–17
13033	Private	Jamieson, A.			19– 7–16
24176	Private	Jennings, J.			10– 3–16
23871	Private	Johnson, D.			4– 4–16
26383	Private	Johnston, E.			17– 3–16
20401	Private	Johnston, J.			16– 8–17
23035	Private	Johnston, T.			13– 3–16
25734	Private	Johnstone, R.			9– 9–16
24669	Private	Jones, E.			9– 9–16
41925	Private	Jones, T.			16– 8–17
27704	Private	Kavanagh, M.			27– 4–16
3368	Private	Kearney, F. J.			28– 4–16
22789	Private	Kearns, J. J.			21– 3–18
27270	Private	Keenan, W.			16– 8–17
16747	Private	Kells, G.	(died at home)		14– 6–15
26497	Private	Kelly, A.			9– 8–17
16393	Sergeant	Kelly, J.	(died at home)		8–11–15
21237	Private	Kelly, J.			9– 8–17
22776	Private	Kelly, J.			6– 9–16
43227	Private	Kelly, J.			16– 8–17
20273	Private	Kelly, M.			27– 4–16
23757	Private	Kelly, P.			4– 4–16
3204	Private	Kennedy, R.			9– 9–16
26255	L/Corpl.	Kenny, A.			9– 9–16
22741	Private	Kerr, J.			16– 8–17
23354	Private	Kyle, A.			28– 4–16
27920	Private	Laidlaw, T.			16– 8–17
26448	Private	Langan, J.			7– 6–17
41192	Private	Langan, M.			8– 8–17
26865	Private	Lannigan, J.			7– 6–17
23438	Private	Lanson, H.			22– 5–16
41638	Private	Laycock, J.			16– 8–17
23671	Private	Lee, J.			27– 4–16

REGIMENTAL NO.	RANK	NAME			DATE
41900	Private	Leicester, J.			16– 8–17
16548	Sergeant	Leslie, J.			27– 4–16
43255	Sergeant	Levy, B.			9– 9–16
41887	Private	Lightfoot, T.			16– 8–17
24124	Private	Lindsay, J.			16– 8–17
41790	Private	Linforth, W. H.			16– 8–17
23668	Private	Little, P.			2– 4–16
26827	Private	Logue, J.			27– 4–16
28630	Private	Love, T.			6– 9–16
41889	Private	Lowe, W.			21– 3–18
26480	Private	McAllister, P.			10– 2–17
23755	Private	McCarron, M.			24– 7–16
27472	Private	McCarron, M.			5– 9–16
27549	Private	McCarthy, J.			4– 4–16
27577	Private	McCauley, P.			27– 4–16
26976	L/Corpl.	McCamley, J.			9– 9–16
27033	Private	McCauley, G.			5– 3–16
21153	Private	McCauley, R.			6– 9–16
20095	Private	McClure, W.			11–11–16
20431	Private	McConckey, J.			6– 4–16
20141	Private	McConnachie, A.			5– 4–16
23973	Private	McCready, R.			27– 4–16
23574	Private	McCrossan, B.			20– 5–16
43216	Private	McCusker, M.			20–10–16
20243	Private	McDaid, J.			7– 6–17
16555	Private	McDaid, G.			6– 4–16
27565	Private	McDonagh, J.			9– 9–16
28623	Private	McHale, M.			16– 9–16
25289	Private	McHugh, M.			20– 5–16
27563	Private	McIlheron, D.			
24526	Corporal	McInally, J.			27– 4–16
18305	Private	McIntosh, J.			7– 8–16
24732	Private	McKeary, W.			8– 9–16
26224	Private	McKee, W.			16– 8–17
21108	Sergeant	McKeman, E., M.M.			16– 8–17
24223	Private	McKemon, P.			7– 6–17
17721	Private	McKinney, D.			16– 6–16
21251	Corporal	McGeehan, J.			9– 9–16
30892	Private	McGlynn, P.			16– 8–17
24175	Private	McGowan, B.			27– 4–16
26488	Private	McGowan, J.			7– 9–16
24705	Private	McGrath, J.			11–11–16
22556	Private	McGrath, M.			16– 8–17
22957	Private	McGratlan, J.			26– 7–17
28634	Private	McHaffie, J.			27– 4–16
28704	Private	McLoughlin, D.			7– 6–17
27475	Private	McManus, F.			31– 5–16
23433	Private	McManus, P.			20– 5–16
16511	Sergeant	McMurray, F. W.			9– 3–16
24301	Private	McNamee, J.			27– 4–16
26987	Private	McNeill, H.			16– 8–17
21111	Private	McShane, W.			16– 8–17
23572	Private	McSorley, E.			16– 8–17
23065	Private	McWilliam, M.			9– 9–16

REGIMENTAL NO.	RANK	NAME			DATE
28693	Private	Madden, P.			27– 4–16
41898	Private	Maddock, J.			30– 3–18
14352	Sergeant	Magee, P.			9– 9–16
41800	Private	Maggs, I. T.			16– 8–17
26514	Private	Maher, P.			19– 7–16
24217	Private	Mallon, P.			9–10–17
41174	Private	Marsh, W. A.			30– 8–17
29799	Private	Martin, H.			21– 3–18
41219	Private	Masterson, R. C.			24–10–18
23981	Private	Mayne, D.			7– 6–17
27343	Private	Mally, D.			24– 7–16
22732	Private	Millar, H.			9– 3–16
26483	Private	Mills, J.			15– 4–16
26452	Private	Moloney, M.			27– 4–16
27852	Private	Monaghan, J.			16– 9–16
26039	L/Corpl.	Montgomery, G.			9– 9–16
23268	Private	Moore, J.			6– 9–16
43218	Private	Moran, A.			9– 9–16
13746	Private	Morgan, M.			10– 3–16
26468	Private	Moriarty, M.			18– 7–16
2467	Private	Morrow, T.			8– 8–17
27824	L/Corpl.	Mulholland, E.			16– 8–17
28621	Private	Mulholland, J.			4– 4–16
13419	Sergeant	Mulholland, W. J.			6– 3–16
27700	Private	Murphy, A.			27– 4–16
27546	Private	Murphy, A.			6– 4–16
43230	Private	Murphy, D.			9– 9–16
14333	Private	Murphy, J.			18–12–17
30147	Private	Murphy, J. J.			16– 8–17
28649	L/Corpl.	Murphy, M.			28– 4 16
27070	Private	Myers, G.			6– 4–16
41795	Private	Nash, F. C.			23– 9–17
49909	Private	Nevins, E.			16– 8–17
21257	Private	Nicholson, C.			18– 8–17
26386	Private	Noble, J. W.			6– 4–16
3286	Private	Nomey, T. J.			16– 7–17
3283	L/Corpl.	North, S.			21– 3–18
26983	Private	O'Connor, B.			9– 5–16
26434	Private	O'Donovan, M.			6– 9–16
26453	Private	O'Hanlon, D.			7– 4–16
26295	Private	O'Hara, D.			9–10–17
23037	Private	O'Kane, F.			27– 4–16
27717	Private	O'Leary, J.			9– 9–16
20502	Private	O'Neill, J.			27– 4–16
28652	Private	O'Neill, P.			16–12–16
26934	Private	O'Neill, R.			21– 3–18
26952	Private	O'Regan, W.			27– 4–16
41194	Private	Orme, W.			16– 8–17
23075	Private	O'Rourke, P.			6– 4–16
25094	Private	O'Toole, L.			27– 4–16
41743	Private	Palmer, G.			16– 8–17
41744	Private	Parham, A.			21– 3–18

REGIMENTAL NO.	RANK	NAME			DATE
20300	Corporal	Parry, R. J.			27– 4–16
28678	L/Sergt.	Pearson, T.			27– 4–16
41746	Private	Perry, F. T.			16– 8–17
1486	Private	Petty, T.			9– 8–17
28848	Private	Poller, J. R.			2– 4–16
28977	Private	Porteous, J.			16– 1–17
22850	Sergeant	Porter, J.			6– 9–16
25290	Private	Porter, P.			27– 4–16
30311	Private	Powell, P. J.			16– 7–18
30314	L/Corpl.	Pratt, F.			16– 8–17
41748	Private	Price, H. E.			16– 8–17
41803	Private	Prior, H.			16– 8–17
24897	Private	Pugh, J. R.			9– 8–17
20851	Corporal	Purdy, G.			27– 4–16
27368	Private	Rafferty, J.			9– 9–16
28695	L/Corpl.	Ramsey, A.			27– 4–16
41749	Private	Read, T. W.			7– 8–17
26952	Private	Regan, W.			————
26108	Private	Reilly, J.			20– 9–16
43297	Private	Reynolds, F.			9– 5–17
42721	Private	Richardson, R. A.			15–10–18
28681	Private	Richardson, J.			6– 4–16
41796	Private	Rigler, C. G.			16– 8–17
19579	Corporal	Robinson, C.			16– 8–17
30315	Private	Roe, J. T.			28–11–18
3390	Corporal	Rosbotham, S.			9– 8–17
23801	Private	Ryan, P. (died at home)			23–12–15
28865	Private	Ryder, P.			12– 7–16
41879	Private	Sanders, A. H.			16– 8–17
27574	L/Corpl.	Savage, M.			9– 9–16
43272	L/Corpl.	Scanlon, J.			16– 8–17
28690	Private	Sheard, O.			6– 9–16
24018	Private	Sheffield, W. J.			5– 4–16
23667	Private	Shields, G.			15– 6–16
23132	Private	Sheridan, J.			28– 5–16
26052	Private	Shields, A.			25– 9–16
18444	L/Corpl.	Smith, J.			7– 6–17
43281	Private	Smith, M.			9– 9–16
24747	Private	Spence, R.			25– 8–16
43232	Private	Stapleton, J.			9– 9–16
30124	Private	Stedman, E.			9– 8–17
43279	Private	Stephens, A. H.			16– 8–17
41821	Private	Stevens, C.			16– 8–17
26477	Private	Storan, E.			27– 4–16
28746	L/Corpl.	Strong, A. E.			16– 8–17
26455	Private	Sullivan, J.			8– 2–17
41199	Private	Sykes, J. R.			16– 8–17
13410	C.S.M.	Taylor, W.			5– 4–16
28625	Corporal	Templeton, J.			27– 4–16
24448	L/Corpl.	Thom, G.			23– 8–17
28582	Private	Thomas, E.			9– 9–16
28552	L/Corpl.	Thomas, T. W.			27– 4–16

23352	Private	Thompson, A.			2– 4–16
41753	Private	Thompson, A. S.			16– 8–17
43190	Private	Tierney, J.			16– 8–17
26954	Private	Tosh, A.			6– 4–16
43274	Private	Tossney, F.			9– 9–16
30322	Private	Tozer, W. J.			7– 6–17
43213	Corporal	Touhy, J.			22– 8–17
23698	L/Corpl.	Turner, J.			16– 8–17
22505	L/Corpl.	Tyrrell, B.			————
23695	Corporal	Upton, T.			26–10–16
41755	Private	Wadron, J. J. V.			10 –8–17
23591	Private	Walker, R.			9– 9–16
26463	L/Corpl.	Walsh, P.			28– 4–16
18306	Private	Ward, P.			27– 4–16
30214	Private	Wells, T.			7– 6–17
30215	Private	Welsh, A. F.			18– 3–17
9272	C.Q.M.S.	Williams, J.			16– 8–17
2363	Private	Williamson, J.			8– 6–17
3523	Private	Williamson, W. J.			9– 9–16
18904	Private	Wilson, J.			9– 9–16
29029	Private	Wilson, R.			16– 8–17
23138	Corporal	Wilson, T.			28– 5–16
27041	Private	Wilson, W.			28– 4–16
22851	Private	Woods, J.			22– 5–16
41648	Private	Wort, A. J.			16– 8–17
20446	L/Sergt.	Wylie, D.			5– 4–16
41662	Private	Yea, H. W.			16– 8–17
26745	Private	Young, J.			6– 4–16

Lightning Source UK Ltd.
Milton Keynes UK
UKOW05f0154130617

303223UK00001B/125/P